GOD

THE INVISIBLE KING

H. G. Wells

God The Invisible King

H. G. Wells

© 1st World Library, 2006
PO Box 2211
Fairfield, IA 52556
www.1stworldlibrary.com
First Edition

LCCN: 2006909915

Softcover ISBN: 978-1-4218-3337-8
Hardcover ISBN: 978-1-4218-3237-1
eBook ISBN: 978-1-4218-3437-5

Purchase *"God The Invisible King"*
as a traditional bound book at:
www.1stWorldLibrary.com/purchase.asp?ISBN=978-1-4218-3337-8

1st World Library is a literary, educational organization dedicated to:

- Creating a free internet library of downloadable ebooks

- Hosting writing competitions and offering book publishing scholarships.

Interested in more 1st World Library books?
contact: literacy@1stworldlibrary.com
Check us out at: www.1stworldlibrary.com

1st World Library Literary Society

Giving Back to the World

"If you want to work on the core problem, it's early school literacy."

— **James Barksdale, former CEO of Netscape**

"No skill is more crucial to the future of a child, or to a democratic and prosperous society, than literacy."

— **Los Angeles Times**

Literacy... means far more than learning how to read and write... The aim is to transmit... knowledge and promote social participation."

— **UNESCO**

"Literacy is not a luxury, it is a right and a responsibility. If our world is to meet the challenges of the twenty-first century we must harness the energy and creativity of all our citizens."

— **President Bill Clinton**

"Parents should be encouraged to read to their children, and teachers should be equipped with all available techniques for teaching literacy, so the varying needs and capacities of individual kids can be taken into account."

— **Hugh Mackay**

CONTENTS

PREFACE 7
1. THE COSMOGONY OF MODERN RELIGION 14
2. HERESIES; OR THE THINGS THAT GOD IS NOT 31
3. THE LIKENESS OF GOD 53
4. THE RELIGION OF ATHEISTS 63
5. THE INVISIBLE KING 84
6. MODERN IDEAS OF SIN AND DAMNATION 119
7. THE IDEA OF A CHURCH 129
THE ENVOY 141

PREFACE

This book sets out as forcibly and exactly as possible the religious belief of the writer. That belief is not orthodox Christianity; it is not, indeed, Christianity at all; its core nevertheless is a profound belief in a personal and intimate God. There is nothing in its statements that need shock or offend anyone who is prepared for the expression of a faith different from and perhaps in several particulars opposed to his own. The writer will be found to be sympathetic with all sincere religious feeling. Nevertheless it is well to prepare the prospective reader for statements that may jar harshly against deeply rooted mental habits. It is well to warn him at the outset that the departure from accepted beliefs is here no vague scepticism, but a quite sharply defined objection to dogmas very widely revered. Let the writer state the most probable occasion of trouble forthwith. An issue upon which this book will be found particularly uncompromising is the dogma of the Trinity. The writer is of opinion that the Council of Nicaea, which forcibly crystallised the controversies of two centuries and formulated the creed upon which all the existing Christian churches are based, was one of the most disastrous and one of the least venerable of all religious gatherings, and he holds that the Alexandrine speculations which were then conclusively imposed upon Christianity merit only disrespectful attention at the present time. There you have a chief possibility of offence. He is quite unable to pretend any awe for what he considers the spiritual monstrosities established by that undignified gathering. He makes no attempt to be obscure or propitiatory in this connection. He criticises the creeds explicitly and frankly, because he believes it is particularly necessary to clear them out of the way of those who are seeking religious consolation at this present time of exceptional religious need. He does little to conceal his indignation at the role played by these dogmas in obscuring, perverting, and preventing the religious life of mankind. After this warning such readers from among the various Christian churches and sects as are accessible to storms of theological fear or passion to whom the Trinity is an ineffable mystery and the name of God almost unspeakably awful, read on at their own risk. This is a religious book written by a believer, but so far as their beliefs and religion go it may seem to them more sceptical and more antagonistic than blank atheism. That the writer cannot tell. He is not simply denying their God. He is declaring that there is a living God, different altogether from that Triune God and nearer to the heart of man. The spirit of this book is like that of a missionary who would only too gladly overthrow and smash some Polynesian divinity of shark's teeth and painted wood and mother-of-pearl. To the writer such elaborations as "begotten of the Father before all worlds" are no better than intellectual shark's teeth and oyster shells. His purpose, like the purpose of that missionary, is not primarily to shock and insult; but he is zealous to liberate, and he is impatient with a reverence that stands between man and God. He gives this fair warning and proceeds with his matter.

His matter is modern religion as he sees it. It is only incidentally and because it is unavoidable that he attacks doctrinal Christianity.

In a previous book, "First and Last Things" (Constable and Co.), he has stated his convictions upon certain general ideas of life and thought as clearly as he could. All of philosophy, all of metaphysics that is, seems to him to be a discussion of the relations of class and individual. The antagonism of the Nominalist and the Realist, the opposition of the One and the Many, the contrast of the Ideal and the Actual, all these oppositions express a certain structural and essential duality in the activity of the human mind. From an imperfect recognition of that duality ensue great masses of misconception. That was the substance of "First and Last Things." In this present book there is no further attack on philosophical or metaphysical questions. Here we work at a less fundamental level and deal with religious feeling and religious ideas. But just as the writer was inclined to attribute a whole world of disputation and inexactitudes to confused thinking about the exact value of classes and terms, so here he is disposed to think that interminable controversies and conflicts arise out of a confusion of intention due to a double meaning of the word "God"; that the word "God" conveys not one idea or set of ideas, but several essentially different ideas, incompatible one with another, and falling mainly into one or other of two divergent groups; and that people slip carelessly from one to the other of these groups of ideas and so get into ultimately inextricable confusions.

The writer believes that the centuries of fluid religious thought that preceded the violent ultimate crystallisation of Nicaea, was essentially a struggle—obscured, of course, by many complexities—to reconcile and get into a relationship these two separate main series of God-ideas.

Putting the leading idea of this book very roughly, these two antagonistic typical conceptions of God may be best contrasted by speaking of one of them as God-as-Nature or the Creator, and of the other as God-as-Christ or the Redeemer. One is the great Outward God; the other is the Inmost God. The first idea was perhaps developed most highly and completely in the God of Spinoza. It is a conception of God tending to pantheism, to an idea of a comprehensive God as ruling with justice rather than affection, to a conception of aloofness and awestriking worshipfulness. The second idea, which is opposed to this idea of an absolute God, is the God of the human heart. The writer would suggest that the great outline of the theological struggles of that phase of civilisation and world unity which produced Christianity, was a persistent but unsuccessful attempt to get these two different ideas of God into one focus. It was an attempt to make the God of Nature accessible and the God of the Heart invincible, to bring the former into a conception of love and to vest the latter with the beauty of stars and flowers and the dignity of inexorable justice. There could be no finer metaphor for such a correlation than Fatherhood and Sonship. But the trouble is that it seems impossible to most people to continue to regard the relations of the Father to the Son as being simply a mystical metaphor. Presently some materialistic bias swings them in a moment of intellectual carelessness back to the idea of sexual filiation.

And it may further be suggested that the extreme aloofness and inhumanity, which is logically necessary in the idea of a Creator God, of an Infinite God, was the reason, so to speak, for the invention of a Holy Spirit, as something proceeding from him, as something bridging the great gulf, a Comforter, a mediator descending into the sphere of the human understanding. That, and the suggestive influence of the Egyptian Trinity that was then being worshipped at the Serapeum, and which had saturated the thought of Alexandria with the conception of a trinity in unity, are probably the realities that account for the Third Person of the Christian Trinity. At any rate the present writer believes that the discussions that shaped the Christian theology we know were dominated by such natural and fundamental thoughts. These discussions were, of course, complicated from the outset; and particularly were they complicated by the identification of the man Jesus with the theological Christ, by materialistic expectations of his second coming, by materialistic inventions about his "miraculous" begetting, and by the morbid speculations about virginity and the like that arose out of such grossness. They were still further complicated by the idea of the textual inspiration of the scriptures, which presently swamped thought in textual interpretation. That swamping came very early in the development of Christianity. The writer of St. John's gospel appears still to be thinking with a considerable freedom, but Origen is already hopelessly in the net of the texts. The writer of St. John's gospel was a free man, but Origen was a superstitious man. He was emasculated mentally as well as bodily through his bibliolatry. He quotes; his predecessor thinks.

But the writer throws out these guesses at the probable intentions of early Christian thought in passing. His business here is the definition of a position. The writer's position here in this book is, firstly, complete Agnosticism in the matter of God the Creator, and secondly, entire faith in the matter of God the Redeemer. That, so to speak, is the key of his book. He cannot bring the two ideas under the same term God. He uses the word God therefore for the God in our hearts only, and he uses the term the Veiled Being for the ultimate mysteries of the universe, and he declares that we do not know and perhaps cannot know in any comprehensible terms the relation of the Veiled Being to that living reality in our lives who is, in his terminology, the true God. Speaking from the point of view of practical religion, he is restricting and defining the word God, as meaning only the personal God of mankind, he is restricting it so as to exclude all cosmogony and ideas of providence from our religious thought and leave nothing but the essentials of the religious life.

Many people, whom one would class as rather liberal Christians of an Arian or Arminian complexion, may find the larger part of this book acceptable to them if they will read "the Christ God" where the writer has written "God." They will then differ from him upon little more than the question whether there is an essential identity in aim and quality between the Christ God and the Veiled Being, who answer to their Creator God. This the orthodox post Nicaean Christians assert, and many pre-Nicaeans and many heretics (as the Cathars) contradicted with its exact contrary. The Cathars, Paulicians, Albigenses and so on held, with the Manichaeans, that the God of Nature, God the Father, was evil. The Christ God was his antagonist. This was the idea of the poet Shelley. And passing beyond Christian theology altogether a clue can still be found to many problems in comparative theology in this distinction between the Being of Nature (cf. Kant's "starry vault above") and the God of the heart (Kant's "moral law within"). The idea of an antagonism seems to have been cardinal in the thought of the Essenes and the Orphic cult and in the Persian dualism. So, too, Buddhism seems to be "antagonistic." On the other hand, the Moslem teaching and modern Judaism seem absolutely to combine and identify the two; God the creator is altogether and without distinction also God the King of Mankind. Christianity stands somewhere between such complete identification and complete antagonism. It admits a difference in attitude between Father and Son in its distinction between the Old Dispensation (of the Old Testament) and the New. Every possible change is rung in the great religions of the world between identification, complete separation, equality, and disproportion of these Beings; but it will be found that these two ideas are, so to speak, the basal elements of all theology in the world. The writer is chary of assertion or denial in these matters. He believes that they are speculations not at all necessary to salvation. He believes that men may differ profoundly in their opinions upon these points and still be in perfect agreement upon the essentials of religion. The reality of religion he believes deals wholly and exclusively with the God of the Heart. He declares as his own opinion, and as the opinion which seems most expressive of modern thought, that there is no reason to suppose the Veiled Being either benevolent or malignant towards men. But if the reader believes that God is Almighty and in every way Infinite the practical outcome is not very different. For the purposes of human relationship it is impossible to deny that God PRESENTS HIMSELF AS FINITE, as struggling and taking a part against evil.

The writer believes that these dogmas of relationship are not merely extraneous to religion, but an impediment to religion. His aim in this book is to give a statement of religion which is no longer entangled in such speculations and disputes.

Let him add only one other note of explanation in this preface, and that is to remark that except for one incidental passage (in Chapter IV., 1), nowhere does he discuss the question of personal immortality. [It is discussed in "First and Last Things," Book IV, 4.] He omits this question because he does not consider that it has any more bearing upon the essentials of religion, than have the theories we may hold about the relation of God and the moral law to the starry universe. The latter is a question for the theologian, the former for the psychologist. Whether we are mortal or immortal, whether the God in our hearts is the Son of or a rebel against the Universe, the reality of religion, the fact of salvation, is still our self-identification with God, irrespective of consequences, and the achievement of his kingdom, in our hearts and in the world. Whether we live forever or die tomorrow does not affect righteousness. Many people seem to find the prospect of a final personal death unendurable. This impresses me as egotism. I have no such appetite for a separate immortality. God is my immortality; what, of me, is identified with God, is God; what is not is of no more permanent value than the snows of yester-year.

H. G. W.

Dunmow, May, 1917.

CHAPTER THE FIRST

THE COSMOGONY OF MODERN RELIGION

1. MODERN RELIGION HAS NO FOUNDER

Perhaps all religions, unless the flaming onset of Mohammedanism be an exception, have dawned imperceptibly upon the world. A little while ago and the thing was not; and then suddenly it has been found in existence, and already in a state of diffusion. People have begun to hear of the new belief first here and then there. It is interesting, for example, to trace how Christianity drifted into the consciousness of the Roman world. But when a religion has been interrogated it has always had hitherto a tale of beginnings, the name and story of a founder. The renascent religion that is now taking shape, it seems, had no founder; it points to no origins. It is the Truth, its believers declare; it has always been here; it has always been visible to those who had eyes to see. It is perhaps plainer than it was and to more people—that is all.

It is as if it still did not realise its own difference. Many of those who hold it still think of it as if it were a kind of Christianity. Some, catching at a phrase of Huxley's, speak of it as Christianity without Theology. They do not know the creed they are carrying. It has, as a matter of fact, a very fine and subtle theology, flatly opposed to any belief that could, except by great stretching of charity and the imagination, be called Christianity. One might find, perhaps, a parallelism with the system ascribed to some Gnostics, but that is far more probably an accidental rather than a sympathetic coincidence. Of that the reader shall presently have an opportunity of judging.

This indefiniteness of statement and relationship is probably only the opening phase of the new faith. Christianity also began with an extreme neglect of definition. It was not at first anything more than a sect of Judaism. It was only after three centuries, amidst the uproar and emotions of the council of Nicaea, when the more enthusiastic Trinitarians stuffed their fingers in their ears in affected horror at the arguments of old Arius, that the cardinal mystery of the Trinity was established as the essential fact of Christianity. Throughout those three centuries, the centuries of its greatest achievements and noblest martyrdoms, Christianity had not defined its God. And even to-day it has to be noted that a large majority of those who possess and repeat the Christian creeds have come into the practice so insensibly from unthinking childhood, that only in the slightest way do they realise the nature of the statements to which they subscribe. They will speak and think of both Christ and God in ways flatly incompatible with the doctrine of the Triune deity upon which, theoretically, the entire fabric of all the churches rests. They will show themselves as frankly Arians as though that damnable heresy had not been washed out of the world forever after centuries of persecution in torrents of blood. But whatever the present state of Christendom in these matters may be, there can be no doubt of the enormous pains taken in the past to give Christian beliefs the exactest, least ambiguous statement possible. Christianity knew itself clearly for what it was in its maturity, whatever the indecisions of its childhood or the confusions of its decay. The renascent religion that one finds now, a thing active and sufficient in many minds, has still scarcely come to self-consciousness. But it is so coming, and this present book is very largely an attempt to state the shape it is assuming and to compare it with the beliefs and imperatives and usages of the various Christian, pseudo-Christian, philosophical, and agnostic cults amidst which it has appeared.

The writer's sympathies and convictions are entirely with this that he speaks of as renascent or modern religion; he is neither atheist nor Buddhist nor Mohammedan nor Christian. He will make no pretence, therefore, to impartiality and detachment. He will do his best to be as fair as possible and as candid as possible, but the reader must reckon with this bias. He has found this faith growing up in himself; he has found it, or something very difficult to distinguish from it, growing independently in the minds of men and women he has met. They have been people of very various origins; English, Americans, Bengalis, Russians, French, people brought up in a "Catholic atmosphere," Positivists, Baptists, Sikhs, Mohammedans. Their diversity of source is as remarkable as their convergence of tendency. A miscellany of minds thinking upon parallel lines has come out to the same light. The new teaching is also traceable in many professedly Christian religious books and it is to be heard from Christian pulpits. The phase of definition is manifestly at hand.

2. MODERN RELIGION HAS A FINITE GOD

Perhaps the most fundamental difference between this new faith and any recognised form of Christianity is that, knowingly or unknowingly, it worships A FINITE GOD. Directly the believer is fairly confronted with the plain questions of the case, the vague identifications that are still carelessly made with one or all of the persons of the Trinity dissolve away. He will admit that his God is neither all-wise, nor all-powerful, nor omnipresent; that he is neither the maker of heaven nor earth, and that he has little to identify him with that hereditary God of the Jews who became the "Father" in the Christian system. On the other hand he will assert that his God is a god of salvation, that he is a spirit, a person, a strongly marked and knowable personality, loving, inspiring, and lovable, who exists or strives to exist in every human soul. He will be much less certain in his denials that his God has a close resemblance to the Pauline (as distinguished from the Trinitarian) "Christ." . . .

The modern religious man will almost certainly profess a kind of universalism; he will assert that whensoever men have called upon any God and have found fellowship and comfort and courage and that sense of God within them, that inner light which is the quintessence of the religious experience, it was the True God that answered them. For the True God is a generous God, not a jealous God; the very antithesis of that bickering monopolist who "will have none other gods but Me"; and when a human heart cries out—to what name it matters not—for a larger spirit and a stronger help than the visible things of life can give, straightway the nameless Helper is with it and the God of Man answers to the call. The True God has no scorn nor hate for those who have accepted the many-handed symbols of the Hindu or the lacquered idols of China. Where there is faith, where there is need, there is the True God ready to clasp the hands that stretch out seeking for him into the darkness behind the ivory and gold.

The fact that God is FINITE is one upon which those who think clearly among the new believers are very insistent. He is, above everything else, a personality, and to be a personality is to have characteristics, to be limited by characteristics; he is a Being, not us but dealing with us and through us, he has an aim and that means he has a past and future; he is within time and not outside it. And they point out that this is really what everyone who prays sincerely to God or gets help from God, feels and believes. Our practice with God is better than our theory. None of us really pray to that fantastic, unqualified danse a trois, the Trinity, which the wranglings and disputes of the worthies of Alexandria and Syria declared to be God. We pray to one single understanding person. But so far the tactics of those Trinitarians at Nicaea, who stuck their fingers in their ears, have prevailed in this world; this was no matter for discussion, they declared, it was a Holy Mystery full of magical terror, and few religious people have thought it worth while to revive these terrors by a definite contradiction. The truly religious have been content to lapse quietly into the comparative sanity of an unformulated Arianism, they have left it to the scoffing Atheist to mock at the patent absurdities of the official creed. But one magnificent protest against this theological fantasy must have been the work of a sincerely religious man, the cold superb humour of that burlesque creed, ascribed, at first no doubt facetiously and then quite seriously, to Saint Athanasius the Great, which, by an irony far beyond its original intention, has become at last the accepted creed of the church.

The long truce in the criticism of Trinitarian theology is drawing to its end. It is when men most urgently need God that they become least patient with foolish presentations and dogmas. The new believers are very definitely set upon a thorough analysis of the nature and growth of the Christian creeds and ideas. There has grown up a practice of assuming that, when God is spoken of, the Hebrew-Christian God of Nicaea is meant. But that God trails with him a thousand misconceptions and bad associations; his alleged infinite nature, his jealousy, his strange preferences, his vindictive Old

Testament past. These things do not even make a caricature of the True God; they compose an altogether different and antagonistic figure.

It is a very childish and unphilosophical set of impulses that has led the theologians of nearly every faith to claim infinite qualities for their deity. One has to remember the poorness of the mental and moral quality of the churchmen of the third, fourth, and fifth centuries who saddled Christendom with its characteristic dogmas, and the extreme poverty and confusion of the circle of ideas within which they thought. Many of these makers of Christianity, like Saint Ambrose of Milan (who had even to be baptised after his election to his bishopric), had been pitchforked into the church from civil life; they lived in a time of pitiless factions and personal feuds; they had to conduct their disputations amidst the struggles of would-be emperors; court eunuchs and favourites swayed their counsels, and popular rioting clinched their decisions. There was less freedom of discussion then in the Christian world than there is at present (1916) in Belgium, and the whole audience of educated opinion by which a theory could be judged did not equal, either in numbers or accuracy of information, the present population of Constantinople. To these conditions we owe the claim that the Christian God is a magic god, very great medicine in battle, "in hoc signo vinces," and the argument so natural to the minds of those days and so absurd to ours, that since he had ALL power, all knowledge, and existed for ever and ever, it was no use whatever to set up any other god against him. . . .

By the fifth century Christianity had adopted as its fundamental belief, without which everyone was to be "damned everlastingly," a conception of God and of Christ's relation to God, of which even by the Christian account of his teaching, Jesus was either totally unaware or so negligent and careless of the future comfort of his disciples as scarcely to make mention. The doctrine of the Trinity, so far as the relationship of the Third Person goes, hangs almost entirely upon one ambiguous and disputed utterance in St. John's gospel (XV. 26). Most of the teachings of Christian orthodoxy resolve themselves to the attentive student into assertions of the nature of contradiction and repartee. Someone floats an opinion in some matter that has been hitherto vague, in regard, for example, to the sonship of Christ or to the method of his birth. The new opinion arouses the hostility and alarm of minds unaccustomed to so definite a statement, and in the zeal of their recoil they fly to a contrary proposition. The Christians would neither admit that they worshipped more gods than one because of the Greeks, nor deny the divinity of Christ because of the Jews. They dreaded to be polytheistic; equally did they dread the least apparent detraction from the power and importance of their Saviour. They were forced into the theory of the Trinity by the necessity of those contrary assertions, and they had to make it a mystery protected by curses to save it from a reductio ad absurdam. The entire history of the growth of the Christian doctrine in those disordered early centuries is a history of theology by committee; a history of furious wrangling, of hasty compromises, and still more hasty attempts to clinch matters by anathema. When the muddle was at its very worst, the church was confronted by enormous political opportunities. In order that it should seize these one chief thing appeared imperative: doctrinal uniformity. The emperor himself, albeit unbaptised and very ignorant of Greek, came and seated himself in the midst of Christian thought upon a golden throne. At the end of it all Eusebius, that supreme Trimmer, was prepared to damn everlastingly all those who doubted that consubstantiality he himself had doubted at the beginning of the conference. It is quite clear that Constantine did not care who was damned or for what period, so long as the Christians ceased to wrangle among themselves. The practical unanimity of Nicaea was secured by threats, and then, turning upon the victors, he sought by threats to restore Arius to communion. The imperial aim was a common faith to unite the empire. The crushing out of the Arians and of the Paulicians and suchlike heretics, and more particularly the systematic destruction by the orthodox of all heretical writings, had about it none of that quality of honest conviction which comes to those who have a real knowledge of God; it was a bawling down of dissensions that, left to work themselves out, would have spoilt good business; it was the fist of Nicolas of Myra over again, except that after the days of Ambrose the sword of the executioner and the fires of the book-burner were added to the weapon of the human voice. Priscillian was the first human sacrifice formally offered up under these improved conditions to the greater glory of the reinforced Trinity. Thereafter the blood of the heretics was the cement of Christian unity.

It is with these things in mind that those who profess the new faith are becoming so markedly anxious to distinguish God from the Trinitarian's deity. At present if anyone who has left the Christian communion declares himself a believer in God, priest and parson swell with self-complacency. There is no reason why they should do so. That many of us have gone from them and found God is no concern of theirs. It is not that we who went out into the wilderness which we thought to be a desert, away from their creeds and dogmas, have turned back and are returning. It is that we have gone on still further, and are beyond that desolation. Never more shall we return to those who gather under the cross. By faith we disbelieved and denied. By faith we said of that stuffed scarecrow of divinity, that incoherent accumulation of antique theological notions, the Nicene deity, "This is certainly no God." And by faith we have found God. . . .

3. THE INFINITE BEING IS NOT GOD

There has always been a demand upon the theological teacher that he should supply a cosmogony. It has always been an effective propagandist thing to say: "OUR God made the whole universe. Don't you think that it would be wise to abandon YOUR deity, who did not, as you admit, do anything of the sort?"

The attentive reader of the lives of the Saints will find that this style of argument did in the past bring many tribes and nations into the Christian fold. It was second only to the claim of magic advantages, demonstrated by a free use of miracles. Only one great religious system, the Buddhist, seems to have resisted the temptation to secure for its divinity the honour and title of Creator. Modern religion is like Buddhism in that respect. It offers no theory whatever about the origin of the universe. It does not reach behind the appearances of space and time. It sees only a featureless presumption in that playing with superlatives which has entertained so many minds from Plotinus to the Hegelians with the delusion that such negative terms as the Absolute or the Unconditioned, can assert anything at all. At the back of all known things there is an impenetrable curtain; the ultimate of existence is a Veiled Being, which seems to know nothing of life or death or good or ill. Of that Being, whether it is simple or complex or divine, we know nothing; to us it is no more than the limit of understanding, the unknown beyond. It may be of practically limitless intricacy and possibility. The new religion does not pretend that the God of its life is that Being, or that he has any relation of control or association with that Being. It does not even assert that God knows all or much more than we do about that ultimate Being.

For us life is a matter of our personalities in space and time. Human analysis probing with philosophy and science towards the Veiled Being reveals nothing of God, reveals space and time only as necessary forms of consciousness, glimpses a dance of atoms, of whirls in the ether. Some day in the endless future there may be a knowledge, an understanding of relationship, a power and courage that will pierce into those black wrappings. To that it may be our God, the Captain of Mankind will take us.

That now is a mere speculation. The veil of the unknown is set with the stars; its outer texture is ether and atom and crystal. The Veiled Being, enigmatical and incomprehensible, broods over the mirror upon which the busy shapes of life are moving. It is as if it waited in a great stillness. Our lives do not deal with it, and cannot deal with it. It may be that they may never be able to deal with it.

4. THE LIFE FORCE IS NOT GOD

So it is that comprehensive setting of the universe presents itself to the modern mind. It is altogether outside good and evil and love and hate. It is outside God, who is love and goodness. And coming out of this veiled being, proceeding out of it in a manner altogether inconceivable, is another lesser being, an impulse thrusting through matter and clothing itself in continually changing material forms, the maker of our world, Life, the Will to Be. It comes out of that inscrutable being as a wave comes rolling to us from beyond the horizon. It is as it were a great wave rushing through matter and possessed by a spirit. It is a breeding, fighting thing; it pants through the jungle track as the tiger and lifts itself towards heaven as the tree; it is the rabbit bolting for its life and the dove calling to her mate; it crawls, it flies, it dives, it lusts and devours, it pursues and eats itself in order to live still more eagerly and hastily; it is every living thing, of it are our passions and desires and fears. And it is aware of itself not as a whole, but dispersedly as individual self-consciousness, starting out dispersedly from every one of the sentient creatures it has called into being. They look out for their little moments, red-eyed and fierce, full of greed, full of the passions of acquisition and assimilation and reproduction, submitting only to brief fellowships of defence or aggression. They are beings of strain and conflict and competition. They are living substance still mingled painfully with the dust. The forms in which this being clothes itself bear thorns and fangs and claws, are soaked with poison and bright with threats or allurements, prey slyly or openly on one another, hold their own for a little while, breed savagely and resentfully, and pass. . . .

This second Being men have called the Life Force, the Will to Live, the Struggle for Existence. They have figured it too as Mother Nature. We may speculate whether it is not what the wiser among the Gnostics meant by the Demiurge, but since the Christians destroyed all the Gnostic books that must remain a mere curious guess. We may speculate whether this heat and haste and wrath of life about us is the Dark God of the Manichees, the evil spirit of the sun worshippers. But in contemporary thought there is no conviction apparent that this Demiurge is either good or evil; it is conceived of as both good and evil. If it gives all the pain and conflict of life, it gives also the joy of the sunshine, the delight and hope of youth, the pleasures. If it has elaborated a hundred thousand sorts of parasite, it has also moulded the beautiful limbs of man and woman; it has shaped the slug and the flower. And in it, as part of it, taking its rewards, responding to its goads, struggling against the final abandonment to death, do we all live, as the beasts live, glad, angry, sorry, revengeful, hopeful, weary, disgusted, forgetful, lustful, happy, excited, bored, in pain, mood after mood but always fearing death, with no certainty and no coherence within us, until we find God. And God comes to us neither out of the stars nor out of the pride of life, but as a still small voice within.

5. GOD IS WITHIN

God comes we know not whence, into the conflict of life. He works in men and through men. He is a spirit, a single spirit and a single person; he has begun and he will never end. He is the immortal part and leader of mankind. He has motives, he has characteristics, he has an aim. He is by our poor scales of measurement boundless love, boundless courage, boundless generosity. He is thought and a steadfast will. He is our friend and brother and the light of the world. That briefly is the belief of the modern mind with regard to God. There is no very novel idea about this God, unless it be the idea that he had a beginning. This is the God that men have sought and found in all ages, as God or as the Messiah or the Saviour. The finding of him is salvation from the purposelessness of life. The new religion has but disentangled the idea of him from the absolutes and infinities and mysteries of the Christian theologians; from mythological virgin births and the cosmogonies and intellectual pretentiousness of a vanished age.

Modern religion appeals to no revelation, no authoritative teaching, no mystery. The statement it makes is, it declares, a mere statement of what we may all perceive and experience. We all live in the storm of life, we all find our understandings limited by the Veiled Being; if we seek salvation and search within for God, presently we find him. All this is in the nature of things. If every one who perceives and states it were to be instantly killed and blotted out, presently other people would find their way to the same conclusions; and so on again and again. To this all true religion, casting aside its hulls of misconception, must ultimately come. To it indeed much religion is already coming. Christian thought struggles towards it, with the millstones of Syrian theology and an outrageous mythology of incarnation and resurrection about its neck. When at last our present bench of bishops join the early fathers of the church in heaven there will be, I fear, a note of reproach in their greeting of the ingenious person who saddled them with OMNIPOTENS. Still more disastrous for them has been the virgin birth, with the terrible fascination of its detail for unpoetic minds. How rich is the literature of authoritative Christianity with decisions upon the continuing virginity of Mary and the virginity of Joseph—ideas that first arose in Arabia as a Moslem gloss upon Christianity—and how little have these peepings and pryings to do with the needs of the heart and the finding of God!

Within the last few years there have been a score or so of such volumes as that recently compiled by Dr. Foakes Jackson, entitled "The Faith and the War," a volume in which the curious reader may contemplate deans and canons, divines and church dignitaries, men intelligent and enquiring and religiously disposed, all lying like overladen camels, panting under this load of obsolete theological responsibility, groaning great articles, outside the needle's eye that leads to God.

6. THE COMING OF GOD

Modern religion bases its knowledge of God and its account of God entirely upon experience. It has encountered God. It does not argue about God; it relates. It relates without any of those wrappings of awe and reverence that fold so necessarily about imposture, it relates as one tells of a friend and his assistance, of a happy adventure, of a beautiful thing found and picked up by the wayside.

So far as its psychological phases go the new account of personal salvation tallies very closely with the account of "conversion" as it is given by other religions. It has little to tell that is not already familiar to the reader of William James's "Varieties of Religious Experience." It describes an initial state of distress with the aimlessness and cruelties of life, and particularly with the futility of the individual life, a state of helpless self-disgust, of inability to form any satisfactory plan of living. This is the common prelude known to many sorts of Christian as "conviction of sin"; it is, at any rate, a conviction of hopeless confusion. . . . Then in some way the idea of God comes into the distressed mind, at first simply as an idea, without substance or belief. It is read about or it is remembered; it is expounded by some teacher or some happy convert. In the case of all those of the new faith with whose personal experience I have any intimacy, the idea of God has remained for some time simply as an idea floating about in a mind still dissatisfied. God is not believed in, but it is realised that if there were such a being he would supply the needed consolation and direction, his continuing purpose would knit together the scattered effort of life, his immortality would take the sting from death. Under this realisation the idea is pursued and elaborated. For a time there is a curious resistance to the suggestion that God is truly a person; he is spoken of preferably by such phrases as the Purpose in Things, as the Racial Consciousness, as the Collective Mind.

I believe that this resistance in so many contemporary minds to the idea of God as a person is due very largely to the enormous prejudice against divine personality created by the absurdities of the Christian teaching and the habitual monopoly of the Christian idea. The picture of Christ as the Good Shepherd thrusts itself before minds unaccustomed to the idea that they are lambs. The cross in the twilight bars the way. It is a novelty and an enormous relief to such people to realise that one may think of God without being committed to think of either the Father, the Son, or the Holy Ghost, or of all of them at once. That freedom had not seemed possible to them. They had been hypnotised and obsessed by the idea that the Christian God is the only thinkable God. They had heard so much about that God and so little of any other. With that release their minds become, as it were, nascent and ready for the coming of God.

Then suddenly, in a little while, in his own time, God comes. This cardinal experience is an undoubting, immediate sense of God. It is the attainment of an absolute certainty that one is not alone in oneself. It is as if one was touched at every point by a being akin to oneself, sympathetic, beyond measure wiser, steadfast and pure in aim. It is completer and more intimate, but it is like standing side by side with and touching someone that we love very dearly and trust completely. It is as if this being bridged a thousand misunderstandings and brought us into fellowship with a great multitude of other people. . . .

"Closer he is than breathing, and nearer than hands and feet."

The moment may come while we are alone in the darkness, under the stars, or while we walk by ourselves or in a crowd, or while we sit and muse. It may come upon the sinking ship or in the tumult of the battle. There is no saying when it may not come to us. . . . But after it has come our lives are changed, God is with us and there is no more doubt of God. Thereafter one goes about the world like one who was lonely and has found a lover, like one who was perplexed and has found a solution. One is assured that there is a Power that fights with us against the confusion and evil within us and without. There comes into the heart an essential and enduring happiness and courage.

There is but one God, there is but one true religious experience, but under a multitude of names, under veils and darknesses, God has in this manner come into countless lives. There is scarcely a faith, however mean and preposterous, that has not been a way to holiness. God who is himself finite, who himself struggles in his great effort from strength to strength, has no spite against error. Far beyond halfway he hastens to meet the purblind. But God is against the darkness in their eyes. The faith which is returning to men girds at veils and shadows, and would see God plainly. It has little respect for mysteries. It rends the veil of the temple in rags and tatters. It has no superstitious fear of this huge friendliness, of this great brother and leader of our little beings. To find God is but the beginning of wisdom, because then for all our days we have to learn his purpose with us and to live our lives with him.

CHAPTER THE SECOND

HERESIES; OR THE THINGS THAT GOD IS NOT

1. HERESIES ARE MISCONCEPTIONS OF GOD

Religion is not a plant that has grown from one seed; it is like a lake that has been fed by countless springs. It is a great pool of living water, mingled from many sources and tainted with much impurity. It is synthetic in its nature; it becomes simpler from original complexities; the sediment subsides.

A life perfectly adjusted to its surroundings is a life without mentality; no judgment is called for, no inhibition, no disturbance of the instinctive flow of perfect reactions. Such a life is bliss, or nirvana. It is unconsciousness below dreaming. Consciousness is discord evoking the will to adjust; it is inseparable from need. At every need consciousness breaks into being. Imperfect adjustments, needs, are the rents and tatters in the smooth dark veil of being through which the light of consciousness shines—the light of consciousness and will of which God is the sun.

So that every need of human life, every disappointment and dissatisfaction and call for help and effort, is a means whereby men may and do come to the realisation of God.

There is no cardinal need, there is no sort of experience in human life from which there does not come or has not come a contribution to men's religious ideas. At every challenge men have to put forth effort, feel doubt of adequacy, be thwarted, perceive the chill shadow of their mortality. At every challenge comes the possibility of help from without, the idea of eluding frustration, the aspiration towards immortality. It is possible to classify the appeals men make for God under the headings of their chief system of effort, their efforts to understand, their fear and their struggles for safety and happiness, the craving of their restlessness for peace, their angers against disorder and their desire for the avenger; their sexual passions and perplexities. . . .

Each of these great systems of needs and efforts brings its own sort of sediment into religion. Each, that is to say, has its own kind of heresy, its distinctive misapprehension of God. It is only in the synthesis and mutual correction of many divergent ideas that the idea of God grows clear. The effort to understand completely, for example, leads to the endless Heresies of Theory. Men trip over the inherent infirmities of the human mind. But in these days one does not argue greatly about dogma. Almost every conceivable error about unity, about personality, about time and quantity and genus and species, about begetting and beginning and limitation and similarity and every kink in the difficult mind of man, has been thrust forward in some form of dogma. Beside the errors of thought are the errors of emotion. Fear and feebleness go straight to the Heresies that God is Magic or that God is Providence; restless egotism at leisure and unchallenged by urgent elementary realities breeds the Heresies of Mysticism, anger and hate call for God's Judgments, and the stormy emotions of sex gave mankind the Phallic God. Those who find themselves possessed by the new spirit in religion, realise very speedily the necessity of clearing the mind of all these exaggerations, transferences, and overflows of feeling. The search for divine truth is like gold washing; nothing is of any value until most has been swept away.

2. HERESIES OF SPECULATION

One sort of heresies stands apart from the rest. It is infinitely the most various sort. It includes all those heresies which result from wrong-headed mental elaboration, as distinguished from those which are the result of hasty and imperfect apprehension, the heresies of the clever rather than the heresies of the obtuse. The former are of endless variety and complexity; the latter are in comparison natural, simple confusions. The former are the errors of the study, the latter the superstitions that spring by the wayside, or are brought down to us in our social structure out of a barbaric past.

To the heresies of thought and speculation belong the elaborate doctrine of the Trinity, dogmas about God's absolute qualities, such odd deductions as the accepted Christian teachings about the virginity of Mary and Joseph, and the like. All these things are parts of orthodox Christianity. Yet none of them did Christ, even by the Christian account, expound or recommend. He treated them as negligible. It was left for the Alexandrians, for Alexander, for little, red-haired, busy, wire-pulling Athanasius to find out exactly what their Master was driving at, three centuries after their Master was dead. . . .

Men still sit at little desks remote from God or life, and rack their inadequate brains to meet fancied difficulties and state unnecessary perfections. They seek God by logic, ignoring the marginal error that creeps into every syllogism. Their conceit blinds them to the limitations upon their thinking. They weave spider-like webs of muddle and disputation across the path by which men come to God. It would not matter very much if it were not that simpler souls are caught in these webs. Every great religious system in the world is choked by such webs; each system has its own. Of all the blood-stained tangled heresies which make up doctrinal Christianity and imprison the mind of the western world to-day, not one seems to have been known to the nominal founder of Christianity. Jesus Christ never certainly claimed to be the Messiah; never spoke clearly of the Trinity; was vague upon the scheme of salvation and the significance of his martyrdom. We are asked to suppose that he left his apostles without instructions, that were necessary to their eternal happiness, that he could give them the Lord's Prayer but leave them to guess at the all-important Creed,* and that the Church staggered along blindly, putting its foot in and out of damnation, until the "experts" of Nicaea, that "garland of priests," marshalled by Constantine's officials, came to its rescue.... From the conversion of Paul onward, the heresies of the intellect multiplied about Christ's memory and hid him from the sight of men. We are no longer clear about the doctrine he taught nor about the things he said and did....

> * Even the "Apostles' Creed" is not traceable earlier than the fourth century. It is manifestly an old, patched formulary. Rutinius explains that it was not written down for a long time, but transmitted orally, kept secret, and used as a sort of password among the elect.

We are all so weary of this theology of the Christians, we are all at heart so sceptical about their Triune God, that it is needless here to spend any time or space upon the twenty thousand different formulae in which the orthodox have attempted to believe in something of the sort. There are several useful encyclopaedias of sects and heresies, compact, but still bulky, to which the curious may go. There are ten thousand different expositions of orthodoxy. No one who really seeks God thinks of the Trinity, either the Trinity of the Trinitarian or the Trinity of the Sabellian or the Trinity of the Arian, any more than one thinks of those theories made stone, those gods with three heads and seven hands, who sit on lotus leaves and flourish lingams and what not, in the temples of India. Let us leave, therefore, these morbid elaborations of the human intelligence to drift to limbo, and come rather to the natural heresies that spring from fundamental weaknesses of the human character, and which are common to all religions. Against these it is necessary to keep constant watch. They return very insidiously.

3. GOD IS NOT MAGIC

One of the most universal of these natural misconceptions of God is to consider him as something magic serving the ends of men.

It is not easy for us to grasp at first the full meaning of giving our souls to God. The missionary and teacher of any creed is all too apt to hawk God for what he will fetch; he is greedy for the poor triumph of acquiescence; and so it comes about that many people who have been led to believe themselves religious, are in reality still keeping back their own souls and trying to use God for their own purposes. God is nothing more for them as yet than a magnificent Fetish. They did not really want him, but they have heard that he is potent stuff; their unripe souls think to make use of him. They call upon his name, they do certain things that are supposed to be peculiarly influential with him, such as saying prayers and repeating gross praises of him, or reading in a blind, industrious way that strange miscellany of Jewish and early Christian literature, the Bible, and suchlike mental mortification, or making the Sabbath dull and uncomfortable. In return for these fetishistic propitiations God is supposed to interfere with the normal course of causation in their favour. He becomes a celestial log-roller. He remedies unfavourable accidents, cures petty ailments, contrives unexpected gifts of medicine, money, or the like, he averts bankruptcies, arranges profitable transactions, and does a thousand such services for his little clique of faithful people. The pious are represented as being constantly delighted by these little surprises, these bouquets and chocolate boxes from the divinity. Or contrawise he contrives spiteful turns for those who fail in their religious attentions. He murders Sabbath-breaking children, or disorganises the careful business schemes of the ungodly. He is represented as going Sabbath-breakering on Sunday morning as a Staffordshire worker goes ratting. Ordinary everyday Christianity is saturated with this fetishistic conception of God. It may be disowned in THE HIBBERT JOURNAL, but it is unblushingly advocated in the parish magazine. It is an idea taken over by Christianity with the rest of the qualities of the Hebrew God. It is natural enough in minds so self-centred that their recognition of weakness and need brings with it no real self-surrender, but it is entirely inconsistent with the modern conception of the true God.

There has dropped upon the table as I write a modest periodical called THE NORTHERN BRITISH ISRAEL REVIEW, illustrated with portraits of various clergymen of the Church of England, and of ladies and gentlemen who belong to the little school of thought which this magazine represents; it is, I should judge, a sub-sect entirely within the Established Church of England, that is to say within the Anglican communion of the Trinitarian Christians. It contains among other papers a very entertaining summary by a gentleman entitled—I cite the unusual title-page of the periodical—"Landseer Mackenzie, Esq.," of the views of Isaiah, Ezekiel, and Obadiah upon the Kaiser William. They are distinctly hostile views. Mr. Landseer Mackenzie discourses not only upon these anticipatory condemnations but also upon the relations of the weather to this war. He is convinced quite simply and honestly that God has been persistently rigging the weather against the Germans. He points out that the absence of mist on the North Sea was of great help to the British in the autumn of 1914, and declares that it was the wet state of the country that really held up the Germans in Flanders in the winter of 1914-15. He ignores the part played by the weather in delaying the relief of Kut-el-Amara, and he has not thought of the difficult question why the Deity, having once decided upon intervention, did not, instead of this comparatively trivial meteorological assistance, adopt the more effective course of, for example, exploding or spoiling the German stores of ammunition by some simple atomic miracle, or misdirecting their gunfire by a sudden local modification of the laws of refraction or gravitation.

Since these views of God come from Anglican vicarages I can only conclude that this kind of belief is quite orthodox and permissible in the established church, and that I am charging orthodox Christianity here with nothing that has ever been officially repudiated. I find indeed the essential assumptions of Mr. Landseer Mackenzie repeated in endless official Christian utterances on the part of German and British and Russian divines. The Bishop of Chelmsford, for example, has recently ascribed our difficulties in the war to our impatience with long sermons—among other similar causes. Such Christians are manifestly convinced that God can be invoked by ritual—for example by special days of national prayer or an increased observance of Sunday—or made malignant by neglect or levity. It is almost fundamental in their idea of him. The ordinary Mohammedan seems as confident of this magic pettiness of God, and the belief of China in the magic propitiations and resentments of "Heaven" is at least equally strong.

But the true God as those of the new religion know him is no such God of luck and intervention. He is not to serve men's ends or the ends of nations or associations of men; he is careless of our ceremonies and invocations. He does not lose his temper with our follies and weaknesses. It is for us to serve Him. He captains us, he does not coddle us. He has his own ends for which he needs us. . . .

4. GOD IS NOT PROVIDENCE

Closely related to this heresy that God is magic, is the heresy that calls him Providence, that declares the apparent adequacy of cause and effect to be a sham, and that all the time, incalculably, he is pulling about the order of events for our personal advantages.

The idea of Providence was very gaily travested by Daudet in "Tartarin in the Alps." You will remember how Tartarin's friend assured him that all Switzerland was one great Trust, intent upon attracting tourists and far too wise and kind to permit them to venture into real danger, that all the precipices were netted invisibly, and all the loose rocks guarded against falling, that avalanches were prearranged spectacles and the crevasses at their worst slippery ways down into kindly catchment bags. If the mountaineer tried to get into real danger he was turned back by specious excuses. Inspired by this persuasion Tartarin behaved with incredible daring. . . . That is exactly the Providence theory of the whole world. There can be no doubt that it does enable many a timid soul to get through life with a certain recklessness. And provided there is no slip into a crevasse, the Providence theory works well. It would work altogether well if there were no crevasses.

Tartarin was reckless because of his faith in Providence, and escaped. But what would have happened to him if he had fallen into a crevasse?

There exists a very touching and remarkable book by Sir Francis Younghusband called "Within." [Williams and Norgate, 1912.] It is the confession of a man who lived with a complete confidence in Providence until he was already well advanced in years. He went through battles and campaigns, he filled positions of great honour and responsibility, he saw much of the life of men, without altogether losing his faith. The loss of a child, an Indian famine, could shake it but not overthrow it. Then coming back one day from some races in

France, he was knocked down by an automobile and hurt very cruelly. He suffered terribly in body and mind. His sufferings caused much suffering to others. He did his utmost to see the hand of a loving Providence in his and their disaster and the torment it inflicted, and being a man of sterling honesty and a fine essential simplicity of mind, he confessed at last that he could not do so. His confidence in the benevolent intervention of God was altogether destroyed. His book tells of this shattering, and how laboriously he reconstructed his religion upon less confident lines. It is a book typical of an age and of a very English sort of mind, a book well worth reading.

That he came to a full sense of the true God cannot be asserted, but how near he came to God, let one quotation witness.

"The existence of an outside Providence," he writes, "who created us, who watches over us, and who guides our lives like a Merciful Father, we have found impossible longer to believe in. But of the existence of a Holy Spirit radiating upward through all animate beings, and finding its fullest expression, in man in love, and in the flowers in beauty, we can be as certain as of anything in the world. This fiery spiritual impulsion at the centre and the source of things, ever burning in us, is the supremely important factor in our existence. It does not always attain to light. In many directions it fails; the conditions are too hard and it is utterly blocked. In others it only partially succeeds. But in a few it bursts forth into radiant light. There are few who in some heavenly moment of their lives have not been conscious of its presence. We may not be able to give it outward expression, but we know that it is there." . . .

God does not guide our feet. He is no sedulous governess restraining and correcting the wayward steps of men. If you would fly into the air, there is no God to bank your aeroplane correctly for you or keep an ill-tended engine going; if you would cross a glacier, no God nor angel guides your steps amidst the slippery places. He will not even mind your innocent children for you if you leave them before an unguarded fire. Cherish no delusions; for yourself and others you challenge danger and chance on your own strength; no talisman, no God, can help you or those you care for. Nothing of such things will God do; it is an idle dream. But God will be with you nevertheless. In the reeling aeroplane or the dark ice-cave God will be your courage. Though you suffer or are killed, it is not an end. He will be with you as you face death; he will die with you as he has died already countless myriads of brave deaths. He will come so close to you that at the last you will not know whether it is you or he who dies, and the present death will be swallowed up in his victory.

5. THE HERESY OF QUIETISM

God comes to us within and takes us for his own. He releases us from ourselves; he incorporates us with his own undying experience and adventure; he receives us and gives himself. He is a stimulant; he makes us live immortally and more abundantly. I have compared him to the sensation of a dear, strong friend who comes and stands quietly beside one, shoulder to shoulder.

The finding of God is the beginning of service. It is not an escape from life and action; it is the release of life and action from the prison of the mortal self. Not to realise that, is the heresy of Quietism, of many mystics. Commonly such people are people of some wealth, able to command services for all their everyday needs. They make religion a method of indolence. They turn their backs on the toil and stresses of existence and give themselves up to a delicious reverie in which they flirt with the divinity. They will recount their privileges and ecstasies, and how ingeniously and wonderfully God has tried and proved them. But indeed the true God was not the lover of Madame Guyon. The true God is not a spiritual troubadour wooing the hearts of men and women to no purpose. The true God goes through the world like fifes and drums and flags, calling for recruits along the street. We must go out to him. We must accept his discipline and fight his battle. The peace of God comes not by thinking about it but by forgetting oneself in him.

6. GOD DOES NOT PUNISH

Man is a social animal, and there is in him a great faculty for moral indignation. Many of the early Gods were mainly Gods of Fear. They were more often "wrath" than not. Such was the temperament of the Semitic deity who, as the Hebrew Jehovah, proliferated, perhaps under the influence of the Alexandrian Serapeum, into the Christian Trinity and who became also the Moslem God.* The natural hatred of unregenerate men against everything that is unlike themselves, against strange people and cheerful people, against unfamiliar usages and things they do not understand, embodied itself in this conception of a malignant and partisan Deity, perpetually "upset" by the little things people did, and contriving murder and vengeance. Now this God would be drowning everybody in the world, now he would be burning Sodom and Gomorrah, now he would be inciting his congenial Israelites to the most terrific pogroms. This divine "frightfulness" is of course the natural human dislike and distrust for queer practices or for too sunny a carelessness, a dislike reinforced by the latent fierceness of the ape in us, liberating the latent fierceness of the ape in us, giving it an excuse and pressing permission upon it, handing the thing hated and feared over to its secular arm. . . .

> * It is not so generally understood as it should be among English and American readers that a very large proportion of early Christians before the creeds established and regularised the doctrine of the Trinity, denied absolutely that Jehovah was God; they regarded Christ as a rebel against Jehovah and a rescuer of humanity from him, just as Prometheus was a rebel against Jove. These beliefs survived for a thousand years throughout Christendom: they were held by a great multitude of persecuted sects, from the Albigenses and Cathars to the eastern Paulicians. The catholic church found it necessary to prohibit the circulation of the Old Testament among laymen very largely on account of the polemics of the Cathars against

the Hebrew God. But in this book, be it noted, the word Christian, when it is not otherwise defined, is used to indicate only the Trinitarians who accept the official creeds.

It is a human paradox that the desire for seemliness, the instinct for restraints and fair disciplines, and the impulse to cherish sweet familiar things, that these things of the True God should so readily liberate cruelty and tyranny. It is like a woman going with a light to tend and protect her sleeping child, and setting the house on fire. None the less, right down to to-day, the heresy of God the Revengeful, God the Persecutor and Avenger, haunts religion. It is only in quite recent years that the growing gentleness of everyday life has begun to make men a little ashamed of a Deity less tolerant and gentle than themselves. The recent literature of the Anglicans abounds in the evidence of this trouble.

Bishop Colenso of Natal was prosecuted and condemned in 1863 for denying the irascibility of his God and teaching "the Kaffirs of Natal" the dangerous heresy that God is all mercy. "We cannot allow it to be said," the Dean of Cape Town insisted, "that God was not angry and was not appeased by punishment." He was angry "on account of Sin, which is a great evil and a great insult to His Majesty." The case of the Rev. Charles Voysey, which occurred in 1870, was a second assertion of the Church's insistence upon the fierceness of her God. This case is not to be found in the ordinary church histories nor is it even mentioned in the latest edition of the ENCYCLOPAEDIA BRITANNICA; nevertheless it appears to have been a very illuminating case. It is doubtful if the church would prosecute or condemn either Bishop Colenso or Mr. Voysey to-day.

7. GOD AND THE NURSERY-MAID

Closely related to the Heresy of God the Avenger, is that kind of miniature God the Avenger, to whom the nursery-maid and the overtaxed parent are so apt to appeal. You stab your children with such a God and he poisons all their lives. For many of us the word "God" first came into our lives to denote a wanton, irrational restraint, as Bogey, as the All-Seeing and quite ungenerous Eye. God Bogey is a great convenience to the nursery-maid who wants to leave Fear to mind her charges and enforce her disciplines, while she goes off upon her own aims. But indeed, the teaching of God Bogey is an outrage upon the soul of a child scarcely less dreadful than an indecent assault. The reason rebels and is crushed under this horrible and pursuing suggestion. Many minds never rise again from their injury. They remain for the rest of life spiritually crippled and debased, haunted by a fear, stained with a persuasion of relentless cruelty in the ultimate cause of all things.

I, who write, was so set against God, thus rendered. He and his Hell were the nightmare of my childhood; I hated him while I still believed in him, and who could help but hate? I thought of him as a fantastic monster, perpetually spying, perpetually listening, perpetually waiting to condemn and to "strike me dead"; his flames as ready as a grill-room fire. He was over me and about my feebleness and silliness and forgetfulness as the sky and sea would be about a child drowning in mid-Atlantic. When I was still only a child of thirteen, by the grace of the true God in me, I flung this Lie out of my mind, and for many years, until I came to see that God himself had done this thing for me, the name of God meant nothing to me but the hideous scar in my heart where a fearful demon had been.

I see about me to-day many dreadful moral and mental cripples with this bogey God of the nursery-maid, with his black, insane revenges, still living like a horrible parasite in their hearts in the place where God should be. They are afraid, afraid, afraid; they dare not be kindly to formal sinners, they dare not abandon a hundred foolish observances; they dare not look at the causes of things. They are afraid of sunshine, of nakedness, of health, of adventure, of science, lest that old watching spider take offence. The voice of the true God whispers in their hearts, echoes in speech and writing, but they avert themselves, fear-driven. For the true God has no lash of fear. And how the foul-minded bigot, with his ill-shaven face, his greasy skin, his thick, gesticulating hands, his bellowings and threatenings, loves to reap this harvest of fear the ignorant cunning of the nursery girl has sown for him! How he loves the importance of denunciation, and, himself a malignant cripple, to rally the company of these crippled souls to persecute and destroy the happy children of God! . . .

Christian priestcraft turns a dreadful face to children. There is a real wickedness of the priest that is different from other wickedness, and that affects a reasonable mind just as cruelty and strange perversions of instinct affect it. Let a former Archbishop of Canterbury speak for me. This that follows is the account given by Archbishop Tait in a debate in the Upper House of Convocation (July 3rd, 1877) of one of the publications of a certain SOCIETY OF THE HOLY CROSS:

"I take this book, as its contents show, to be meant for the instruction of very young children. I find, in one of the pages of it, the statement that between the ages of six and six and a half years would be the proper time for the inculcation of the teaching which is to be found in the book. Now, six to six and a half is certainly a very tender age, and to these children I find these statements addressed in the book:

"It is to the priest, and to the priest only, that the child must acknowledge his sins, if he desires that God should forgive him."

"I hope and trust the person, the three clergymen, or however many there were, did not exactly realise what they were writing; that they did not mean to say that a child was not to confess its sins to God direct; that it was not to confess its sins, at the age of six, to its mother, or to its father, but was only to have recourse to the priest. But the words, to say the least of them, are rash. Then comes the very obvious question:

"Do you know why? It is because God, when he was on earth, gave to his priests, and to them alone, the Divine Power of forgiving men their sins. It was to priests alone that Jesus said: "Receive ye the Holy Ghost." . . . Those who will not confess will not be cured. Sin is a terrible sickness, and casts souls into hell."

"That is addressed to a child six years of age."

"'I have known,' the book continues, poor children who concealed their sins in confession for years; they were very unhappy, were tormented with remorse, and if they had died in that state they would certainly have gone to the everlasting fires of hell." . . .

Now here is something against nature, something that I have seen time after time in the faces and bearing of priests and heard in their preaching. It is a distinct lust. Much nobility and devotion there are among priests, saintly lives and kindly lives, lives of real worship, lives no man may better; this that I write is not of all, perhaps not of many priests. But there has been in all ages that have known sacerdotalism this terrible type of the priest; priestcraft and priestly power release an aggressive and narrow disposition to a recklessness of suffering and a hatred of liberty that surely exceeds the badness of any other sort of men.

8. THE CHILDREN'S GOD

Children do not naturally love God. They have no great capacity for an idea so subtle and mature as the idea of God. While they are still children in a home and cared for, life is too kind and easy for them to feel any great need of God. All things are still something God-like. . . .

The true God, our modern minds insist upon believing, can have no appetite for unnatural praise and adoration. He does not clamour for the attention of children. He is not like one of those senile uncles who dream of glory in the nursery, who love to hear it said, "The children adore him." If children are loved and trained to truth, justice, and mutual forbearance, they will be ready for the true God as their needs bring them within his scope. They should be left to their innocence, and to their trust in the innocence of the world, as long as they can be. They should be told only of God as a Great Friend whom some day they will need more and understand and know better. That is as much as most children need. The phrases of religion put too early into their mouths may become a cant, something worse than blasphemy.

Yet children are sometimes very near to God. Creative passion stirs in their play. At times they display a divine simplicity. But it does not follow that therefore they should be afflicted with theological formulae or inducted into ceremonies and rites that they may dislike or misinterpret. If by any accident, by the death of a friend or a distressing story, the thought of death afflicts a child, then he may begin to hear of God, who takes those that serve him out of their slain bodies into his shining immortality. Or if by some menial treachery, through some prowling priest, the whisper of Old Bogey reaches our children, then we may set their minds at ease by the assurance of his limitless charity. . . .

With adolescence comes the desire for God and to know more

of God, and that is the most suitable time for religious talk and teaching.

9. GOD IS NOT SEXUAL

In the last two or three hundred years there has been a very considerable disentanglement of the idea of God from the complex of sexual thought and feeling. But in the early days of religion the two things were inseparably bound together; the fury of the Hebrew prophets, for example, is continually proclaiming the extraordinary "wrath" of their God at this or that little dirtiness or irregularity or breach of the sexual tabus. The ceremony of circumcision is clearly indicative of the original nature of the Semitic deity who developed into the Trinitarian God. So far as Christianity dropped this rite, so far Christianity disavowed the old associations. But to this day the representative Christian churches still make marriage into a mystical sacrament, and, with some exceptions, the Roman communion exacts the sacrifice of celibacy from its priesthood, regardless of the mischievousness and maliciousness that so often ensue. Nearly every Christian church inflicts as much discredit and injustice as it can contrive upon the illegitimate child. They do not treat illegitimate children as unfortunate children, but as children with a mystical and an incurable taint of SIN. Kindly easy-going Christians may resent this statement because it does not tally with their own attitudes, but let them consult their orthodox authorities.

One must distinguish clearly here between what is held to be sacred or sinful in itself and what is held to be one's duty or a nation's duty because it is in itself the wisest, cleanest, clearest, best thing to do. By the latter tests and reasonable arguments most or all of our institutions regulating the relations of the sexes may be justifiable. But my case is not whether they can be justified by these tests but that it is not by these tests that they are judged even to-day, by the professors of the chief religions of the world. It is the temper and not the conclusions of the religious bodies that I would criticise. These sexual questions are guarded by a holy irascibility, and the most violent efforts are made—with a sense of complete righteousness—to prohibit their discussion. That fury about sexual things is only to be explained on the hypothesis that the Christian God remains a sex God in the minds of great numbers of his exponents. His disentanglement from that plexus is incomplete. Sexual things are still to the orthodox Christian, sacred things.

Now the God whom those of the new faith are finding is only mediately concerned with the relations of men and women. He is no more sexual essentially than he is essentially dietetic or hygienic. The God of Leviticus was all these things. He is represented as prescribing the most petty and intimate of observances—many of which are now habitually disregarded by the Christians who profess him. . . . It is part of the evolution of the idea of God that we have now so largely disentangled our conception of him from the dietary and regimen and meticulous sexual rules that were once inseparably bound up with his majesty. Christ himself was one of the chief forces in this disentanglement, there is the clearest evidence in several instances of his disregard of the rule and his insistence that his disciples should seek for the spirit underlying and often masked by the rule. His Church, being made of baser matter, has followed him as reluctantly as possible and no further than it was obliged. But it has followed him far enough to admit his principle that in all these matters there is no need for superstitious fear, that the interpretation of the divine purpose is left to the unembarrassed intelligence of men. The church has followed him far enough to make the harsh threatenings of priests and ecclesiastics against what they are pleased to consider impurity or sexual impiety, a profound inconsistency. One seems to hear their distant protests when one reads of Christ and the Magdalen, or of Christ eating with publicans and sinners. The clergy of our own days play the part of the New Testament Pharisees with the utmost exactness and complete unconsciousness. One cannot imagine a modern ecclesiastic conversing with a Magdalen in terms of ordinary civility, unless she was in a very high social position indeed, or blending with disreputable characters without a dramatic sense of condescension and much explanatory by-play. Those who profess modern religion do but follow in these matters a course entirely compatible with what has survived of the authentic teachings of Christ, when they declare that God is not sexual, and that religious passion and insult and persecution upon the score of sexual things are a barbaric inheritance.

But lest anyone should fling off here with some hasty assumption that those who profess the religion of the true God are sexually anarchistic, let stress be laid at once upon the opening sentence of the preceding paragraph, and let me a little anticipate a section which follows. We would free men and women from exact and superstitious rules and observances, not to make them less the instruments of God but more wholly his. The claim of modern religion is that one should give oneself unreservedly to God, that there is no other salvation. The believer owes all his being and every moment of his life to God, to keep mind and body as clean, fine, wholesome, active and completely at God's service as he can. There is no scope for indulgence or dissipation in such a consecrated life. It is a matter between the individual and his conscience or his doctor or his social understanding what exactly he may do or not do, what he may eat or drink or so forth, upon any occasion. Nothing can exonerate him from doing his utmost to determine and perform the right act. Nothing can excuse his failure to do so. But what is here being insisted upon is that none of these things has immediately to do with God or religious emotion, except only the general will to do right in God's service. The detailed interpretation of that "right" is for the dispassionate consideration of the human intelligence.

All this is set down here as distinctly as possible. Because of the emotional reservoirs of sex, sexual dogmas are among the most obstinately recurrent of all heresies, and sexual excitement is always tending to leak back into religious feeling. Amongst the sex-tormented priesthood of the Roman communion in particular, ignorant of the extreme practices of the Essenes and of the Orphic cult and suchlike predecessors of Christianity, there seems to be an extraordinary belief that chastity was not invented until Christianity came, and that the religious life is largely the propitiation of God by feats of sexual abstinence. But a superstitious abstinence that scars and embitters the mind, distorts the imagination, makes the body gross and keeps it unclean, is just as offensive to God as any positive depravity.

CHAPTER THE THIRD

THE LIKENESS OF GOD

1. GOD IS COURAGE

Now having set down what those who profess the new religion regard as the chief misconceptions of God, having put these systems of ideas aside from our explanations, the path is cleared for the statement of what God is. Since language springs entirely from material, spatial things, there is always an element of metaphor in theological statement. So that I have not called this chapter the Nature of God, but the Likeness of God.

And firstly, GOD IS COURAGE.

2. GOD IS A PERSON

And next GOD IS A PERSON.

Upon this point those who are beginning to profess modern religion are very insistent. It is, they declare, the central article, the axis, of their religion. God is a person who can be known as one knows a friend, who can be served and who receives service, who partakes of our nature; who is, like us, a being in conflict with the unknown and the limitless and the forces of death; who values much that we value and is against much that we are pitted against. He is our king to whom we must be loyal; he is our captain, and to know him is to have a direction in our lives. He feels us and knows us; he is helped and gladdened by us. He hopes and attempts. . . . God is no abstraction nor trick of words, no Infinite. He is as real as a bayonet thrust or an embrace.

Now this is where those who have left the old creeds and come asking about the new realisations find their chief difficulty. They say, Show us this person; let us hear him. (If they listen to the silences within, presently they will hear him.) But when one argues, one finds oneself suddenly in the net of those ancient controversies between species and individual, between the one and the many, which arise out of the necessarily imperfect methods of the human mind. Upon these matters there has been much pregnant writing during the last half century. Such ideas as this writer has to offer are to be found in a previous little book of his, "First and Last Things," in which, writing as one without authority or specialisation in logic and philosophy, as an ordinary man vividly interested, for others in a like case, he was at some pains to elucidate the imperfections of this instrument of ours, this mind, by which we must seek and explain and reach up to God. Suffice it here to say that theological discussion may very easily become like the vision of a man with cataract, a mere projection of inherent imperfections. If we do not use our phraseology with a certain courage, and take that of those who are trying to convey their ideas to us with a certain politeness and charity, there is no end possible to any discussion in so subtle and intimate a matter as theology but assertions, denials, and wranglings. And about this word "person" it is necessary to be as clear and explicit as possible, though perfect clearness, a definition of mathematical sharpness, is by the very nature of the case impossible.

Now when we speak of a person or an individual we think typically of a man, and we forget that he was once an embryo and will presently decay; we forget that he came of two people and may beget many, that he has forgotten much and will forget more, that he can be confused, divided against himself, delirious, drunken, drugged, or asleep. On the contrary we are, in our hasty way of thinking of him, apt to suppose him continuous, definite, acting consistently and never forgetting. But only abstract and theoretical persons are like that. We couple with him the idea of a body. Indeed, in the common use of the word "person" there is more thought of body than of mind. We speak of a lover possessing the person of his mistress. We speak of offences against the person as opposed to insults, libels, or offences against property. And the gods of primitive men and the earlier civilisations were quite of that quality of person. They were thought of as living in very splendid bodies and as acting consistently. If they were invisible in the ordinary world it was because they were aloof or because their "persons" were too splendid for weak human eyes. Moses was permitted a mitigated view of the person of the Hebrew God on Mount Horeb; and Semele, who insisted upon seeing Zeus in the glories that were sacred to Juno, was utterly consumed. The early Islamic conception of God, like the conception of most honest, simple Christians to-day, was clearly, in spite of the theologians, of a very exalted anthropomorphic personality away somewhere in Heaven. The personal appearance of the Christian God is described in The Revelation, and however much that description may be explained away by commentators as symbolical, it is certainly taken by most straightforward believers as a statement of concrete reality. Now if we are going to insist upon this primary meaning of person and individual, then certainly God as he is now conceived is not a person and not an individual. The true God will never promenade an Eden or a Heaven, nor sit upon a throne.

But current Christianity, modern developments of Islam, much Indian theological thought—that, for instance, which has found such delicate and attractive expression in the devotional poetry of Rabindranath Tagore—has long since abandoned this anthropomorphic insistence upon a body. From the earliest ages man's mind has found little or no difficulty in the idea of something essential to the personality, a soul or a spirit or both, existing apart from the body and continuing after the destruction of the body, and being still a person and an individual. From this it is a small step to the thought of a person existing independently of any existing or pre-existing body. That is the idea of theological Christianity, as distinguished from the Christianity of simple faith. The Triune Persons—omnipresent, omniscient, and omnipotent—exist for all time, superior to and independent of matter. They are supremely disembodied. One became incarnate—as a wind eddy might take up a whirl of dust. . . . Those who profess modern religion conceive that this is an excessive abstraction of the idea of spirituality, a disembodiment of the idea of personality beyond the limits of the conceivable; nevertheless they accept the conception that a person, a spiritual individual, may be without an ordinary mortal body. . . . They declare that God is without any specific body, that he is immaterial, that he can affect the material universe—and that means that he can only reach our sight, our hearing, our touch—through the bodies of those who believe in him and serve him.

His nature is of the nature of thought and will. Not only has he, in his essence, nothing to do with matter, but nothing to do with space. He is not of matter nor of space. He comes into them. Since the period when all the great theologies that prevail to-day were developed, there have been great changes in the ideas of men towards the dimensions of time and space. We owe to Kant the release from the rule of these ideas as essential ideas. Our modern psychology is alive to the possibility of Being that has no extension in space at all, even as our speculative geometry can entertain the possibility of dimensions—fourth, fifth, Nth dimensions—outside the three-dimensional universe of our experience. And God being non-spatial is not thereby banished to an infinite remoteness, but brought nearer to us; he is everywhere immediately at hand, even as a fourth dimension would be everywhere immediately at hand. He is a Being of the minds and in the minds of men. He is in immediate contact with all who apprehend him. . . .

But modern religion declares that though he does not exist in matter or space, he exists in time just as a current of thought may do; that he changes and becomes more even as a man's purpose gathers itself together; that somewhere in the dawning of mankind he had a beginning, an awakening, and that as mankind grows he grows. With our eyes he looks out upon the universe he invades; with our hands, he lays hands upon it. All our truth, all our intentions and achievements, he gathers to himself. He is the undying human memory, the increasing human will.

But this, you may object, is no more than saying that God is the collective mind and purpose of the human race. You may declare that this is no God, but merely the sum of mankind. But those who believe in the new ideas very steadfastly deny that. God is, they say, not an aggregate but a synthesis. He is not merely the best of all of us, but a Being in himself, composed of that but more than that, as a temple is more than a gathering of stones, or a regiment is more than an accumulation of men. They point out that a man is made up of a great multitude of cells, each equivalent to a unicellular organism. Not one of those cells is he, nor is he simply just the addition of all of them. He is more than all of them. You can take away these and these and these, and he still remains. And he can detach part of himself and treat it as if it were not himself, just as a man may beat his breast or, as Cranmer the martyr did, thrust his hand into the flames. A man is none the less himself because his hair is cut or his appendix removed or his leg amputated.

And take another image. . . . Who bears affection for this or that spadeful of mud in my garden? Who cares a throb of the heart for all the tons of chalk in Kent or all the lumps of limestone in Yorkshire? But men love England, which is made up of such things.

And so we think of God as a synthetic reality, though he has neither body nor material parts. And so too we may obey him and listen to him, though we think but lightly of the men whose hands or voices he sometimes uses. And we may think of him as having moods and aspects—as a man has—and a consistency we call his character.

These are theorisings about God. These are statements to convey this modern idea of God. This, we say, is the nature of the person whose will and thoughts we serve. No one, however, who understands the religious life seeks conversion by argument. First one must feel the need of God, then one must form or receive an acceptable idea of God. That much is no more than turning one's face to the east to see the coming of the sun. One may still doubt if that direction is the east or whether the sun will rise. The real coming of God is not that. It is a change, an irradiation of the mind. Everything is there as it was before, only now it is aflame. Suddenly the light fills one's eyes, and one knows that God has risen and that doubt has fled for ever.

3. GOD IS YOUTH

The third thing to be told of the true God is that GOD IS YOUTH.

God, we hold, began and is always beginning. He looks forever into the future.

Most of the old religions derive from a patriarchal phase. God is in those systems the Ancient of Days. I know of no Christian attempt to represent or symbolise God the Father which is not a bearded, aged man. White hair, beard, bearing, wrinkles, a hundred such symptoms of senile decay are there. These marks of senility do not astonish our modern minds in the picture of God, only because tradition and usage have blinded our eyes to the absurdity of a time-worn immortal. Jove too and Wotan are figures far past the prime of their vigour. These are gods after the ancient habit of the human mind, that turned perpetually backward for causes and reasons and saw all things to come as no more than the working out of Fate,—

> "Of Man's first disobedience and the fruit
> Of that forbidden tree, whose mortal taste
> Brought death into the world and all our woe."

But the God of this new age, we repeat, looks not to our past but our future, and if a figure may represent him it must be the figure of a beautiful youth, already brave and wise, but hardly come to his strength. He should stand lightly on his feet in the morning time, eager to go forward, as though he had but newly arisen to a day that was still but a promise; he should bear a sword, that clean, discriminating weapon, his eyes should be as bright as swords; his lips should fall apart with eagerness for the great adventure before him, and he should be in very fresh and golden harness, reflecting the rising sun. Death should still hang like mists and cloud banks and shadows in the valleys of the wide landscape about him. There should be dew upon the threads of gossamer and little leaves and blades of the turf at his feet. . . .

4. WHEN WE SAY GOD IS LOVE

One of the sayings about God that have grown at the same time most trite and most sacred, is that God is Love. This is a saying that deserves careful examination. Love is a word very loosely used; there are people who will say they love new potatoes; there are a multitude of loves of different colours and values. There is the love of a mother for her child, there is the love of brothers, there is the love of youth and maiden, and the love of husband and wife, there is illicit love and the love one bears one's home or one's country, there are dog-lovers and the loves of the Olympians, and love which is a passion of jealousy. Love is frequently a mere blend of appetite and preference; it may be almost pure greed; it may have scarcely any devotion nor be a whit self-forgetful nor generous. It is possible so to phrase things that the furtive craving of a man for another man's wife may be made out to be a light from God. Yet about all the better sorts of love, the sorts of love that people will call "true love," there is something of that same exaltation out of the narrow self that is the essential quality of the knowledge of God.

Only while the exaltation of the love passion comes and goes, the exaltation of religious passion comes to remain. Lovers are the windows by which we may look out of the prison of self, but God is the open door by which we freely go. And God never dies, nor disappoints, nor betrays.

The love of a woman and a man has usually, and particularly in its earlier phases of excitement, far too much desire, far too much possessiveness and exclusiveness, far too much distrust or forced trust, and far too great a kindred with jealousy to be like the love of God. The former is a dramatic relationship that drifts to a climax, and then again seeks presently a climax, and that may be satiated or fatigued. But the latter is far more like the love of comrades, or like the love of a man and a woman who have loved and been through much trouble together, who have hurt one another and forgiven, and come to a complete and generous fellowship. There is a strange and beautiful love that men tell of that will spring up on battlefields between sorely wounded men, and often they are men who have fought together, so that they will do almost incredibly brave and tender things for one another, though but recently they have been trying to kill each other. There is often a pure exaltation of feeling between those who stand side by side manfully in any great stress. These are the forms of love that perhaps come nearest to what we mean when we speak of the love of God.

That is man's love of God, but there is also something else; there is the love God bears for man in the individual believer. Now this is not an indulgent, instinctive, and sacrificing love like the love of a woman for her baby. It is the love of the captain for his men; God must love his followers as a great captain loves his men, who are so foolish, so helpless in themselves, so confiding, and yet whose faith alone makes him possible. It is an austere love. The spirit of God will not hesitate to send us to torment and bodily death. . . .

And God waits for us, for all of us who have the quality to reach him. He has need of us as we of him. He desires us and desires to make himself known to us. When at last the individual breaks through the limiting darknesses to him, the irradiation of that moment, the smile and soul clasp, is in God as well as in man. He has won us from his enemy. We come staggering through into the golden light of his kingdom, to fight for his kingdom henceforth, until at last we are altogether taken up into his being.

CHAPTER THE FOURTH

THE RELIGION OF ATHEISTS

1. THE SCIENTIFIC ATHEIST

It is a curious thing that while most organised religions seem to drape about and conceal and smother the statement of the true God, the honest Atheist, with his passionate impulse to strip the truth bare, is constantly and unwittingly reproducing the divine likeness. It will be interesting here to call a witness or so to the extreme instability of absolute negation.

Here, for example, is a deliverance from Professor Metchnikoff, who was a very typical antagonist of all religion. He died only the other day. He was a very great physiologist indeed; he was a man almost of the rank and quality of Pasteur or Charles Darwin. A decade or more ago he wrote a book called "The Nature of Man," in which he set out very plainly a number of illuminating facts about life. They are facts so illuminating that presently, in our discussion of sin, they will be referred to again. But it is not Professor Metchnikoff's intention to provide material for a religious discussion. He sets out his facts in order to overthrow theology as he conceives it. The remarkable thing about his book, the thing upon which I would now lay stress, is that he betrays no inkling of the fact that he has no longer the right to conceive theology as he conceives it. The development of his science has destroyed that right.

He does not realise how profoundly modern biology has affected our ideas of individuality and species, and how the import of theology is modified through these changes. When he comes from his own world of modern biology to religion and philosophy he goes back in time. He attacks religion as he understood it when first he fell out with it fifty years or more ago.

Let us state as compactly as possible the nature of these changes that biological science has wrought almost imperceptibly in the general scheme and method of our thinking.

The influence of biology upon thought in general consists essentially in diminishing the importance of the individual and developing the realisation of the species, as if it were a kind of super-individual, a modifying and immortal super-individual, maintaining itself against the outer universe by the birth and death of its constituent individuals. Natural History, which began by putting individuals into species as if the latter were mere classificatory divisions, has come to see that the species has its adventures, its history and drama, far exceeding in interest and importance the individual adventure. "The Origin of Species" was for countless minds the discovery of a new romance in life.

The contrast of the individual life and this specific life may be stated plainly and compactly as follows. A little while ago we current individuals, we who are alive now, were each of us distributed between two parents, then between four grand-parents, and so on backward, we are temporarily assembled, as it were, out of an ancestral diffusion; we stand our trial, and presently our individuality is dispersed and mixed again with other individualities in an uncertain multitude of descendants. But the species is not like this; it goes on steadily from newness to newness, remaining still a unity. The drama of the individual life is a mere episode, beneficial or abandoned, in this continuing adventure of the species. And Metchnikoff finds most of the trouble of life and the distresses of life in the fact that the species is still very painfully adjusting itself to the fluctuating conditions under which it lives. The conflict of life is a continual pursuit of adjustment, and the "ills of life," of the individual life that is, are due to its "disharmonies." Man, acutely aware of himself as an individual adventure and unawakened to himself as a species, finds life jangling and distressful, finds death frustration. He fails and falls as a person in what may be the success and triumph of his kind. He does not apprehend the struggle or the nature of victory, but only his own gravitation to death and personal extinction.

Now Professor Metchnikoff is anti-religious, and he is anti-religious because to him as to so many Europeans religion is confused with priest-craft and dogmas, is associated with disagreeable early impressions of irrational repression and misguidance. How completely he misconceives the quality of religion, how completely he sees it as an individual's affair, his own words may witness:

"Religion is still occupied with the problem of death. The solutions which as yet it has offered cannot be regarded as satisfactory. A future life has no single argument to support it, and the non-existence of life after death is in consonance with the whole range of human knowledge. On the other hand, resignation as preached by Buddha will fail to satisfy humanity, which has a longing for life, and is overcome by the thought of the inevitability of death."

Now here it is clear that by death he means the individual death, and by a future life the prolongation of individuality. But Buddhism does not in truth appear ever to have been concerned with that, and modern religious developments are certainly not under that preoccupation with the narrower self. Buddhism indeed so far from "preaching resignation" to death, seeks as its greater good a death so complete as to be absolute release from the individual's burthen of KARMA. Buddhism seeks an ESCAPE FROM INDIVIDUAL IMMORTALITY. The deeper one pursues religious thought the more nearly it approximates to a search for escape from the self-centred life and over-individuation, and the more it diverges from

Professor Metchnikoff's assertion of its aims. Salvation is indeed to lose one's self. But Professor Metchnikoff having roundly denied that this is so, is then left free to take the very essentials of the religious life as they are here conceived and present them as if they were the antithesis of the religious life. His book, when it is analysed, resolves itself into just that research for an escape from the painful accidents and chagrins of individuation, which is the ultimate of religion.

At times, indeed, he seems almost wilfully blind to the true solution round and about which his writing goes. He suggests as his most hopeful satisfaction for the cravings of the human heart, such a scientific prolongation of life that the instinct for self-preservation will be at last extinct. If that is not the very "resignation" he imputes to the Buddhist I do not know what it is. He believes that an individual which has lived fully and completely may at last welcome death with the same instinctive readiness as, in the days of its strength, it shows for the embraces of its mate. We are to be glutted by living to six score and ten. We are to rise from the table at last as gladly as we sat down. We shall go to death as unresistingly as tired children go to bed. Men are to have a life far beyond the range of what is now considered their prime, and their last period (won by scientific self-control) will be a period of ripe wisdom (from seventy to eighty to a hundred and twenty or thereabouts) and public service!

(But why, one asks, public service? Why not book-collecting or the simple pleasure of reminiscence so dear to aged egotists? Metchnikoff never faces that question. And again, what of the man who is challenged to die for right at the age of thirty? What does the prolongation of life do for him? And where are the consolations for accidental misfortune, for the tormenting disease or the lost limb?)

But in his peroration Professor Metchnikoff lapses into pure religiosity. The prolongation of life gives place to sheer self-sacrifice as the fundamental "remedy." And indeed what other remedy has ever been conceived for the general evil of life?

"On the other hand," he writes, "the knowledge that the goal of human life can be attained only by the development of a high degree of solidarity amongst men will restrain actual egotism. The mere fact that the enjoyment of life according to the precepts of Solomon (Ecelesiastes ix. 7-10)* is opposed to the goal of human life, will lessen luxury and the evil that comes from luxury. Conviction that science alone is able to redress the disharmonies of the human constitution will lead directly to the improvement of education and to the solidarity of mankind.

> * Go thy way, eat thy bread with joy, and drink thy wine with a merry heart; for God now accepteth thy works. Let thy garments be always white; and let thy head lack no ointment. Live joyfully with the wife whom thou lovest all the days of the life of thy vanity, which he hath given thee under the sun, all the days of thy vanity for that is thy portion in this life, and in thy labour which thou takest under the sun. Whatsoever thy hand findeth to do, do it with thy might; for there is no work, nor device, nor knowledge, nor wisdom, in the grave, whither thou goest.

"In progress towards the goal, nature will have to be consulted continuously. Already, in the case of the ephemerids, nature has produced a complete cycle of normal life ending in natural death. In the problem of his own fate, man must not be content with the gifts of nature; he must direct them by his own efforts. Just as he has been able to modify the nature of animals and plants, man must attempt to modify his own constitution, so as to readjust its disharmonies. . . .

"To modify the human constitution, it will be necessary first, to frame the ideal, and thereafter to set to work with all the resources of science.

"If there can be formed an ideal able to unite men in a kind of religion of the future, this ideal must be founded on scientific principles. And if it be true, as has been asserted so often, that man can live by faith alone, the faith must be in the power of science."

Now this, after all the flat repudiations that have preceded it of "religion" and "philosophy" as remedies for human ills, is nothing less than the fundamental proposition of the religious life translated into terms of materialistic science, the proposition that damnation is really over-individuation and that salvation is escape from self into the larger being of life. . . .

What can this "religion of the future" be but that devotion to the racial adventure under the captaincy of God which we have already found, like gold in the bottom of the vessel, when we have washed away the confusions and impurities of dogmatic religion? By an inquiry setting out from a purely religious starting-point we have already reached conclusions identical with this ultimate refuge of an extreme materialist.

This altar to the Future of his, we can claim as an altar to our God—an altar rather indistinctly inscribed.

2. SACRIFICE IMPLIES GOD

Almost all Agnostic and Atheistical writings that show any fineness and generosity of spirit, have this tendency to become as it were the statement of an anonymous God. Everything is said that a religious writer would say—except that God is not named. Religious metaphors abound. It is as if they accepted the living body of religion but denied the bones that held it together—as they might deny the bones of a friend. It is true, they would admit, the body moves in a way that implies bones in its every movement, but—WE HAVE NEVER SEEN THOSE BONES.

The disputes in theory—I do not say the difference in reality—between the modern believer and the atheist or agnostic—becomes at times almost as impalpable as that subtle discussion dear to students of physics, whether the scientific "ether" is real or a formula. Every material phenomenon is consonant with and helps to define this ether, which permeates and sustains and is all things, which nevertheless is perceptible to no sense, which is reached only by an intellectual process. Most minds are disposed to treat this ether as a reality. But the acutely critical mind insists that what is only so attainable by inference is not real; it is no more than "a formula that satisfies all phenomena."

But if it comes to that, am I anything more than the formula that satisfies all my forms of consciousness?

Intellectually there is hardly anything more than a certain will to believe, to divide the religious man who knows God to be utterly real, from the man who says that God is merely a formula to satisfy moral and spiritual phenomena. The former has encountered him, the other has as yet felt only unassigned impulses. One says God's will is so; the other that Right is so. One says God moves me to do this or that; the other the Good Will in me which I share with you and all well-disposed men, moves me to do this or that. But the former makes an exterior reference and escapes a risk of self-righteousness.

I have recently been reading a book by Mr. Joseph McCabe called "The Tyranny of Shams," in which he displays very typically this curious tendency to a sort of religion with God "blacked out." His is an extremely interesting case. He is a writer who was formerly a Roman Catholic priest, and in his reaction from Catholicism he displays a resolution even sterner than Professor Metchnikoff's, to deny that anything religious or divine can exist, that there can be any aim in life except happiness, or any guide but "science." But—and here immediately he turns east again—he is careful not to say "individual happiness." And he says "Pleasure is, as Epicureans insisted, only a part of a large ideal of happiness." So he lets the happiness of devotion and sacrifice creep in. So he opens indefinite possibilities of getting away from any merely materialistic rule of life. And he writes:

"In every civilised nation the mass of the people are inert and indifferent. Some even make a pretence of justifying their inertness. Why, they ask, should we stir at all? Is there such a thing as a duty to improve the earth? What is the meaning or purpose of life? Or has it a purpose?

"One generally finds that this kind of reasoning is merely a piece of controversial athletics or a thin excuse for idleness. People tell you that the conflict of science and religion—it would be better to say, the conflict of modern culture and ancient traditions—has robbed life of its plain significance. The men who, like Tolstoi, seriously urge this point fail to appreciate the modern outlook on life. Certainly modern culture—science, history, philosophy, and art—finds no purpose in life: that is to say, no purpose eternally fixed and to be discovered by man. A great chemist said a few years ago that he could imagine 'a series of lucky accidents'—the chance blowing by the wind of certain chemicals into pools on the primitive earth—accounting for the first appearance of life; and one might not unjustly sum up the influences which have lifted those early germs to the level of conscious beings as a similar series of lucky accidents.

"But it is sheer affectation to say that this demoralises us. If there is no purpose impressed on the universe, or prefixed to the development of humanity, it follows only that humanity may choose its own purpose and set up its own goal; and the most elementary sense of order will teach us that this choice must be social, not merely individual. In whatever measure ill-controlled individuals may yield to personal impulses or attractions, the aim of the race must be a collective aim. I do not mean an austere demand of self-sacrifice from the individual, but an adjustment—as genial and generous as possible—of individual variations for common good. Otherwise life becomes discordant and futile, and the pain and waste react on each individual. So we raise again, in the twentieth century, the old question of 'the greatest good,' which men discussed in the Stoa Poikile and the suburban groves of Athens, in the cool atria of patrician mansions on the Palatine and the Pincian, in the Museum at Alexandria, and the schools which Omar Khayyam frequented, in the straw-strewn schools of the Middle Ages and the opulent chambers of Cosimo dei Medici."

And again:

"The old dream of a co-operative effort to improve life, to bring happiness to as many minds of mortals as we can reach, shines above all the mists of the day. Through the ruins of creeds and philosophies, which have for ages disdained it, we are retracing our steps toward that height—just as the Athenians did two thousand years ago. It rests on no metaphysic, no sacred legend, no disputable tradition—nothing that scepticism can corrode or advancing knowledge undermine. Its foundations are the fundamental and unchanging impulses of our nature."

And again:

"The revolt which burns in so much of the abler literature of our time is an unselfish revolt, or non-selfish revolt: it is an outcome of that larger spirit which conceives the self to be a part of the general social organism, and it is therefore neither egoistic nor altruistic. It finds a sanction in the new intelligence, and an inspiration in the finer sentiments of our generation, but the glow which chiefly illumines it is the glow of the great vision of a happier earth. It speaks of the claims of truth and justice, and assails untruth and injustice, for these are elemental principles of social life; but it appeals more confidently to the warmer sympathy which is linking the scattered children of the race, and it urges all to co-operate in the restriction of suffering and the creation of happiness. The advance guard of the race, the men and women in whom mental alertness is associated with fine feeling, cry that they have reached Pisgah's slope and in increasing numbers men and women are pressing on to see if it be really the Promised Land."

"Pisgah—the Promised Land!" Mr. McCabe in that passage sounds as if he were half-way to "Oh! Beulah Land!" and the tambourine.

That "larger spirit," we maintain, is God; those "impulses" are the power of God, and Mr. McCabe serves a Master he denies. He has but to realise fully that God is not necessarily the Triune God of the Catholic Church, and banish his intense suspicion that he may yet be lured back to that altar he abandoned, he has but to look up from that preoccupation, and immediately he will begin to realise the presence of Divinity.

3. GOD IS AN EXTERNAL REALITY

It may be argued that if atheists and agnostics when they set themselves to express the good will that is in them, do shape out God, that if their conception of right living falls in so completely with the conception of God's service as to be broadly identical, then indeed God, like the ether of scientific speculation, is no more than a theory, no more than an imaginative externalisation of man's inherent good will. Why trouble about God then? Is not the declaration of a good disposition a sufficient evidence of salvation? What is the difference between such benevolent unbelievers as Professor Metchnikoff or Mr. McCabe and those who have found God?

The difference is this, that the benevolent atheist stands alone upon his own good will, without a reference, without a standard, trusting to his own impulse to goodness, relying upon his own moral strength. A certain immodesty, a certain self-righteousness, hangs like a precipice above him; incalculable temptations open like gulfs beneath his feet. He has not really given himself or got away from himself. He has no one to whom he can give himself. He is still a masterless man. His exaltation is self-centred, is priggishness, his fall is unrestrained by any exterior obligation. His devotion is only the good will in himself, a disposition; it is a mood that may change. At any moment it may change. He may have pledged himself to his own pride and honour, but who will hold him to his bargain? He has no source of strength beyond his own amiable sentiments, his conscience speaks with an unsupported voice, and no one watches while he sleeps. He cannot pray; he can but ejaculate. He has no real and living link with other men of good will.

And those whose acquiescence in the idea of God is merely intellectual are in no better case than those who deny God altogether. They may have all the forms of truth and not divinity. The religion of the atheist with a God-shaped blank at its heart and the persuasion of the unconverted theologian, are both like lamps unlit. The lit lamp has no difference in form from the lamp unlit. But the lit lamp is alive and the lamp unlit is asleep or dead.

The difference between the unconverted and the unbeliever and the servant of the true God is this; it is that the latter has experienced a complete turning away from self. This only difference is all the difference in the world. It is the realisation that this goodness that I thought was within me and of myself and upon which I rather prided myself, is without me and above myself, and infinitely greater and stronger than I. It is the immortal and I am mortal. It is invincible and steadfast in its purpose, and I am weak and insecure. It is no longer that I, out of my inherent and remarkable goodness, out of the excellence of my quality and the benevolence of my heart, give a considerable amount of time and attention to the happiness and welfare of others—because I choose to do so. On the contrary I have come under a divine imperative, I am obeying an irresistible call, I am a humble and willing servant of the righteousness of God. That altruism which Professor Metchnikoff and Mr. McCabe would have us regard as the goal and refuge of a broad and free intelligence, is really the first simple commandment in the religious life.

4. ANOTHER RELIGIOUS MATERIALIST

Now here is a passage from a book, "Evolution and the War," by Professor Metchnikoff's translator, Dr. Chalmers Mitchell, which comes even closer to our conception of God as an immortal being arising out of man, and external to the individual man. He has been discussing that well-known passage of Kant's: "Two things fill my mind with ever-renewed wonder and awe the more often and deeper I dwell on them—the starry vault above me, and the moral law within me."

From that discussion, Dr. Chalmers Mitchell presently comes to this most definite and interesting statement:

"Writing as a hard-shell Darwinian evolutionist, a lover of the scalpel and microscope, and of patient, empirical observation, as one who dislikes all forms of supernaturalism, and who does not shrink from the implications even of the phrase that thought is a secretion of the brain as bile is a secretion of the liver, I assert as a biological fact that the moral law is as real and as external to man as the starry vault. It has no secure seat in any single man or in any single nation. It is the work of the blood and tears of long generations of men. It is not in man, inborn or innate, but is enshrined in his traditions, in his customs, in his literature and his religion. Its creation and sustenance are the crowning glory of man, and his consciousness of it puts him in a high place above the animal world. Men live and die; nations rise and fall, but the struggle of individual lives and of individual nations must be measured not by their immediate needs, but as they tend to the debasement or perfection of man's great achievement."

This is the same reality. This is the same Link and Captain that this book asserts. It seems to me a secondary matter whether we call Him "Man's Great Achievement" or "The Son of Man" or the "God of Mankind" or "God." So far as the practical and moral ends of life are concerned, it does not matter how we explain or refuse to explain His presence in our lives.

There is but one possible gap left between the position of Dr. Chalmers Mitchell and the position of this book. In this book it is asserted that GOD RESPONDS, that he GIVES courage and the power of self-suppression to our weakness.

5. A NOTE ON A LECTURE BY PROFESSOR GILBERT MURRAY

Let me now quote and discuss a very beautiful passage from a lecture upon Stoicism by Professor Gilbert Murray, which also displays the same characteristic of an involuntary shaping out of God in the forms of denial. It is a passage remarkable for its conscientious and resolute Agnosticism. And it is remarkable too for its blindness to the possibility of separating quite completely the idea of the Infinite Being from the idea of God. It is another striking instance of that obsession of modern minds by merely Christian theology of which I have already complained. Professor Murray has quoted Mr. Bevan's phrase for God, "the Friend behind phenomena," and he does not seem to realise that that phrase carries with it no obligation whatever to believe that this Friend is in control of the phenomena. He assumes that he is supposed to be in control as if it were a matter of course:

"We do seem to find," Professor Murray writes, "not only in all religions, but in practically all philosophies, some belief that man is not quite alone in the universe, but is met in his endeavours towards the good by some external help or sympathy. We find it everywhere in the unsophisticated man. We find it in the unguarded self-revelations of the most severe and conscientious Atheists. Now, the Stoics, like many other schools of thought, drew an argument from this consensus of all mankind. It was not an absolute proof of the existence of the Gods or Providence, but it was a strong indication. The existence of a common instinctive belief in the mind of man gives at least a presumption that there must be a good cause for that belief.

"This is a reasonable position. There must be some such cause. But it does not follow that the only valid cause is the truth of the content of the belief. I cannot help suspecting that this is precisely one of those points on which Stoicism, in company with almost all philosophy up to the present time, has gone astray through not sufficiently realising its dependence on the human mind as a natural biological product. For it is very important in this matter to realise that the so-called belief is not really an intellectual judgment so much as a craving of the whole nature.

"It is only of very late years that psychologists have begun to realise the enormous dominion of those forces in man of which he is normally unconscious. We cannot escape as easily as these brave men dreamed from the grip of the blind powers beneath the threshold. Indeed, as I see philosophy after philosophy falling into this unproven belief in the Friend behind phenomena, as I find that I myself cannot, except for a moment and by an effort, refrain from making the same assumption, it seems to me that perhaps here too we are under the spell of a very old ineradicable instinct. We are gregarious animals; our ancestors have been such for countless ages. We cannot help looking out on the world as gregarious animals do; we see it in terms of humanity and of fellowship. Students of animals under domestication have shown us how the habits of a gregarious creature, taken away from his kind, are shaped in a thousand details by reference to the lost pack which is no longer there—the pack which a dog tries to smell his way back to all the time he is out walking, the pack he calls to for help when danger threatens. It is a strange and touching thing, this eternal hunger of the gregarious animal for the herd of friends who are not there. And it may be, it may very possibly be, that, in the matter of this Friend behind phenomena our own yearning and our own almost ineradicable instinctive conviction, since they are certainly not founded on either reason or observation, are in origin the groping of a lonely-souled gregarious animal to find its herd or its herd-leader in the great spaces between the stars.

"At any rate, it is a belief very difficult to get rid of."

There the passage and the lecture end.

I would urge that here again is an inadvertent witness to the reality of God.

Professor Murray writes of gregarious animals as though there existed solitary animals that are not gregarious, pure individualists, "atheists" so to speak, and as though this appeal to a life beyond one's own was not the universal disposition of living things. His classical training disposes him to a realistic exaggeration of individual difference. But nearly every animal, and certainly every mentally considerable animal, begins under parental care, in a nest or a litter, mates to breed, and is associated for much of its life. Even the great carnivores do not go alone except when they are old and have done with the most of life. Every pack, every herd, begins at some point in a couple, it is the equivalent of the tiger's litter if that were to remain undispersed. And it is within the memory of men still living that in many districts the African lion has with a change of game and conditions lapsed from a "solitary" to a gregarious, that is to say a prolonged family habit of life.

Man too, if in his ape-like phase he resembled the other higher apes, is an animal becoming more gregarious and not less. He has passed within the historical period from a tribal gregariousness to a nearly cosmopolitan tolerance. And he has his tribe about him. He is not, as Professor Murray seems to suggest, a solitary LOST gregarious beast. Why should his desire for God be regarded as the overflow of an unsatisfied gregarious instinct, when he has home, town, society, companionship, trade union, state, INCREASINGLY at hand to glut it? Why should gregariousness drive a man to God rather than to the third-class carriage and the public-house? Why should gregariousness drive men out of crowded Egyptian cities into the cells of the Thebaid? Schopenhauer in a memorable passage (about the hedgehogs who assembled for warmth) is flatly opposed to Professor Murray, and seems far more plausible when he declares that the nature of man is insufficiently gregarious. The parallel with the dog is not a valid one.

Does not the truth lie rather in the supposition that it is not the Friend that is the instinctive delusion but the isolation? Is not the real deception, our belief that we are completely individualised, and is it not possible that this that Professor Murray calls "instinct" is really not a vestige but a new thing arising out of our increasing understanding, an intellectual penetration to that greater being of the species, that vine, of which we are the branches? Why should not the soul of the species, many faceted indeed, be nevertheless a soul like our own?

Here, as in the case of Professor Metchnikoff, and in many other cases of atheism, it seems to me that nothing but an inadequate understanding of individuation bars the way to at least the intellectual recognition of the true God.

6. RELIGION AS ETHICS

And while I am dealing with rationalists, let me note certain recent interesting utterances of Sir Harry Johnston's. You will note that while in this book we use the word "God" to indicate the God of the Heart, Sir Harry uses "God" for that idea of God-of-the-Universe, which we have spoken of as the Infinite Being. This use of the word "God" is of late theological origin; the original identity of the words "good" and "god" and all the stories of the gods are against him. But Sir Harry takes up God only to define him away into incomprehensible necessity. Thus:

"We know absolutely nothing concerning the Force we call God; and, assuming such an intelligent ruling force to be in existence, permeating this universe of millions of stars and (no doubt) tens of millions of planets, we do not know under what conditions and limitations It works. We are quite entitled to assume that the end of such an influence is intended to be order out of chaos, happiness and perfection out of incompleteness and misery; and we are entitled to identify the reactionary forces of brute Nature with the anthropomorphic Devil of primitive religions, the power of darkness resisting the power of light. But in these conjectures we must surely come to the conclusion that the theoretical potency we call 'God' makes endless experiments, and scrap-heaps the failures. Think of the Dinosaurs and the expenditure of creative energy that went to their differentiation and their well-nigh incredible physical development. . . .

"To such a Divine Force as we postulate, the whole development and perfecting of life on this planet, the whole production of man, may seem little more than to any one of us would be the chipping out, the cutting, the carving, and the polishing of a gem; and we should feel as little remorse or pity for the scattered dust and fragments as must the Creative Force of the immeasurably vast universe feel for the DISJECTA MEMBRA of perfected life on this planet. . . ."

But thence he goes on to a curiously imperfect treatment of the God of man as if he consisted in nothing more than some vague sort of humanitarianism. Sir Harry's ideas are much less thoroughly thought out than those of any other of these sceptical writers I have quoted. On that account they are perhaps more typical. He speaks as though Christ were simply an eminent but ill-reported and abominably served teacher of ethics—and yet of the only right ideal and ethics. He speaks as though religions were nothing more than ethical movements, and as though Christianity were merely someone remarking with a bright impulsiveness that everything was simply horrid, and so, "Let us instal loving kindness as a cardinal axiom." He ignores altogether the fundamental essential of religion, which is THE DEVELOPMENT AND SYNTHESIS OF THE DIVERGENT AND CONFLICTING MOTIVES OF THE UNCONVERTED LIFE, AND THE IDENTIFICATION OF THE INDIVIDUAL LIFE WITH THE IMMORTAL PURPOSE OF GOD. He presents a conception of religion relieved of its "nonsense" as the cheerful self-determination of a number of bright little individuals (much stirred but by no means overcome by Cosmic Pity) to the Service of Man. As he seems to present it, it is as outward a thing, it goes as little into the intimacy of their lives, as though they had after proper consideration agreed to send a subscription to a Red Cross Ambulance or take part in a public demonstration against the Armenian Massacres, or do any other rather nice-spirited exterior thing. This is what he says:

"I hope that the religion of the future will devote itself wholly to the Service of Man. It can do so without departing from the Christian ideal and Christian ethics. It need only drop all that is silly and disputable, and 'mattering not neither here nor there,' of Christian theology—a theology virtually absent from the direct teaching of Christ—and all of Judaistic literature or prescriptions not made immortal in their application by unassailable truth and by the confirmation of science. An excellent remedy for the nonsense which still clings about religion may be found in two books: Cotter Monson's 'Service of Man,' which was published as long ago as 1887, and has since been re-issued by the Rationalist Press Association in its well-known sixpenny series, and J. Allanson Picton's 'Man and the Bible.' Similarly, those who wish to acquire a sane view of the relations between man and God would do well to read Winwood Reade's 'Martyrdom of Man.'"

Sir Harry in fact clears the ground for God very ably, and then makes a well-meaning gesture in the vacant space. There is no help nor strength in his gesture unless God is there. Without God, the "Service of Man" is no better than a hobby or a sentimentality or an hypocrisy in the undisciplined prison of the mortal life.

CHAPTER THE FIFTH

THE INVISIBLE KING

1. MODERN RELIGION A POLITICAL RELIGION

The conception of a young and energetic God, an Invisible Prince growing in strength and wisdom, who calls men and women to his service and who gives salvation from self and mortality only through self-abandonment to his service, necessarily involves a demand for a complete revision and fresh orientation of the life of the convert.

God faces the blackness of the Unknown and the blind joys and confusions and cruelties of Life, as one who leads mankind through a dark jungle to a great conquest. He brings mankind not rest but a sword. It is plain that he can admit no divided control of the world he claims. He concedes nothing to Caesar. In our philosophy there are no human things that are God's and others that are Caesar's. Those of the new thought cannot render unto God the things that are God's, and to Caesar the things that are Caesar's. Whatever claim Caesar may make to rule men's lives and direct their destinies outside the will of God, is a usurpation. No king nor Caesar has any right to tax or to service or to tolerance, except he claim as one who holds for and under God. And he must make good his claim. The steps of the altar of the God of Youth are no safe place for the sacrilegious figure of a king. Who claims "divine right" plays with the lightning.

The new conceptions do not tolerate either kings or aristocracies or democracies. Its implicit command to all its adherents is to make plain the way to the world theocracy. Its rule of life is the discovery and service of the will of God, which dwells in the hearts of men, and the performance of that will, not only in the private life of the believer but in the acts and order of the state and nation of which he is a part. I give myself to God not only because I am so and so but because I am mankind. I become in a measure responsible for every evil in the world of men. I become a knight in God's service. I become my brother's keeper. I become a responsible minister of my King. I take sides against injustice, disorder, and against all those temporal kings, emperors, princes, landlords, and owners, who set themselves up against God's rule and worship. Kings, owners, and all who claim rule and decisions in the world's affairs, must either show themselves clearly the fellow-servants of the believer or become the objects of his steadfast antagonism.

2. THE WILL OF GOD

It is here that those who explain this modern religiosity will seem most arbitrary to the inquirer. For they relate of God, as men will relate of a close friend, his dispositions, his apparent intentions, the aims of his kingship. And just as they advance no proof whatever of the existence of God but their realisation of him, so with regard to these qualities and dispositions they have little argument but profound conviction. What they say is this; that if you do not feel God then there is no persuading you of him; we cannot win over the incredulous. And what they say of his qualities is this; that if you feel God then you will know, you will realise more and more clearly, that thus and thus and no other is his method and intention.

It comes as no great shock to those who have grasped the full implications of the statement that God is Finite, to hear it asserted that the first purpose of God is the attainment of clear knowledge, of knowledge as a means to more knowledge, and of knowledge as a means to power. For that he must use human eyes and hands and brains.

And as God gathers power he uses it to an end that he is only beginning to apprehend, and that he will apprehend more fully as time goes on. But it is possible to define the broad outlines of the attainment he seeks. It is the conquest of death.

It is the conquest of death; first the overcoming of death in the individual by the incorporation of the motives of his life into an undying purpose, and then the defeat of that death that seems to threaten our species upon a cooling planet beneath a cooling sun. God fights against death in every form, against the great death of the race, against the petty death of indolence, insufficiency, baseness, misconception, and perversion. He it is and no other who can deliver us "from the body of this death." This is the battle that grows plainer; this is the purpose to which he calls us out of the animal's round of eating, drinking, lusting, quarrelling and laughing and weeping, fearing and failing, and presently of wearying and dying, which is the whole life that living without God can give us. And from these great propositions there follow many very definite maxims and rules of life for those who serve God. These we will immediately consider.

3. THE CRUCIFIX

But first let me write a few words here about those who hold a kind of intermediate faith between the worship of the God of Youth and the vaguer sort of Christianity. There are a number of people closely in touch with those who have found the new religion who, biased probably by a dread of too complete a break with Christianity, have adopted a theogony which is very reminiscent of Gnosticism and of the Paulician, Catharist, and kindred sects to which allusion has already been made. He, who is called in this book God, they would call God-the-Son or Christ, or the Logos; and what is here called the Darkness or the Veiled Being, they would call God-the-Father. And what we speak of here as Life, they would call, with a certain disregard of the poor brutes that perish, Man. And they would assert, what we of the new belief, pleading our profound ignorance, would neither assert nor deny, that that Darkness, out of which came Life and God, since it produced them must be ultimately sympathetic and of like nature with them. And that ultimately Man, being redeemed and led by Christ and saved from death by him, would be reconciled with God the Father.* And this great adventurer out of the hearts of man that we here call God, they would present as the same with that teacher from Galilee who was crucified at Jerusalem.

> * This probably was the conception of Spinoza. Christ for him is the wisdom of God manifested in all things, and chiefly in the mind of man. Through him we reach the blessedness of an intuitive knowledge of God. Salvation is an escape from the "inadequate" ideas of the mortal human personality to the "adequate" and timeless ideas of God.

Now we of the modern way would offer the following criticisms upon this apparent compromise between our faith and the current religion. Firstly, we do not presume to theorise about the nature of the veiled being nor about that being's relations to God and to Life. We do not recognise any consistent sympathetic possibilities between these outer beings and our God. Our God is, we feel, like Prometheus, a rebel. He is unfilial. And the accepted figure of Jesus, instinct with meek submission, is not in the tone of our worship. It is not by suffering that God conquers death, but by fighting. Incidentally our God dies a million deaths, but the thing that matters is not the deaths but the immortality. It may be he cannot escape in this person or that person being nailed to a cross or chained to be torn by vultures on a rock. These may be necessary sufferings, like hunger and thirst in a campaign; they do not in themselves bring victory. They may be necessary, but they are not glorious. The symbol of the crucifixion, the drooping, pain-drenched figure of Christ, the sorrowful cry to his Father, "My God, my God, why hast thou forsaken me?" these things jar with our spirit. We little men may well fail and repent, but it is our faith that our God does not fail us nor himself. We cannot accept the Christian's crucifix, or pray to a pitiful God. We cannot accept the Resurrection as though it were an after-thought to a bitterly felt death. Our crucifix, if you must have a crucifix, would show God with a hand or a foot already torn away from its nail, and with eyes not downcast but resolute against the sky; a face without pain, pain lost and forgotten in the surpassing glory of the struggle and the inflexible will to live and prevail. . . .

But we do not care how long the thorns are drawn, nor how terrible the wounds, so long as he does not droop. God is courage. God is courage beyond any conceivable suffering.

But when all this has been said, it is well to add that it concerns the figure of Christ only in so far as that professes to be the figure of God, and the crucifix only so far as that stands for divine action. The figure of Christ crucified, so soon as we think of it as being no more than the tragic memorial of Jesus, of the man who proclaimed the loving-kindness of God and the supremacy of God's kingdom over the individual life, and who, in the extreme agony of his pain and exhaustion, cried out that he was deserted, becomes something altogether distinct from a theological symbol. Immediately that we cease to worship, we can begin to love and pity. Here was a being of extreme gentleness and delicacy and of great courage, of the utmost tolerance and the subtlest sympathy, a saint of non-resistance. . . .

We of the new faith repudiate the teaching of non-resistance. We are the militant followers of and participators in a militant God. We can appreciate and admire the greatness of Christ, this gentle being upon whose nobility the theologians trade. But submission is the remotest quality of all from our God, and a moribund figure is the completest inversion of his likeness as we know him. A Christianity which shows, for its daily symbol, Christ risen and trampling victoriously upon a broken cross, would be far more in the spirit of our worship.*

> * It is curious, after writing the above, to find in a letter written by Foss Westcott, Bishop of Durham, to that pertinacious correspondent, the late Lady Victoria Welby, almost exactly the same sentiments I have here expressed. "If I could fill the Crucifix with life as you do," he says, "I would gladly look on it, but the fallen Head and the closed Eye exclude from my thought the idea of glorified humanity. The Christ to whom we are led is One who 'hath been crucified,' who hath passed the trial victoriously and borne the fruits to heaven. I dare not then rest on this side of the glory."

I find, too, a still more remarkable expression of the modern spirit in a tract, "The Call of the Kingdom," by that very able and subtle, Anglican theologian, the Rev. W. Temple, who declares that under the vitalising stresses of the war we are winning "faith in Christ as an heroic leader. We have thought of Him so much as meek and gentle that there is no ground in our picture of Him, for the vision which His disciple had of Him: 'His head and His hair were white, as white wool, white as snow; and His eyes were as a flame of fire: and His feet like unto burnished brass, as if it had been refined in a furnace; and His voice was as the voice of many waters. And He had in His right hand seven stars; and out of His mouth proceeded a sharp two-edged sword; and His countenance was as the sun shineth in its strength.'"

These are both exceptional utterances, interesting as showing how clearly parallel are the tendencies within and without Christianity.

4. THE PRIMARY DUTIES

Now it follows very directly from the conception of God as a finite intelligence of boundless courage and limitless possibilities of growth and victory, who has pitted himself against death, who stands close to our inmost beings ready to receive us and use us, to rescue us from the chagrins of egotism and take us into his immortal adventure, that we who have realised him and given ourselves joyfully to him, must needs be equally ready and willing to give our energies to the task we share with him, to do our utmost to increase knowledge, to increase order and clearness, to fight against indolence, waste, disorder, cruelty, vice, and every form of his and our enemy, death, first and chiefest in ourselves but also in all mankind, and to bring about the establishment of his real and visible kingdom throughout the world.

And that idea of God as the Invisible King of the whole world means not merely that God is to be made and declared the head of the world, but that the kingdom of God is to be present throughout the whole fabric of the world, that the Kingdom of God is to be in the teaching at the village school, in the planning of the railway siding of the market town, in the mixing of the mortar at the building of the workman's house. It means that ultimately no effigy of intrusive king or emperor is to disfigure our coins and stamps any more; God himself and no delegate is to be represented wherever men buy or sell, on our letters and our receipts, a perpetual witness, a perpetual reminder. There is no act altogether without significance, no power so humble that it may not be used for or against God, no life but can orient itself to him. To realise God in one's heart is to be filled with the desire to serve him, and the way of his service is neither to pull up one's life by the roots nor to continue it in all its essentials unchanged, but to turn it about, to turn everything that there is in it round into his way.

The outward duty of those who serve God must vary greatly

with the abilities they possess and the positions in which they find themselves, but for all there are certain fundamental duties; a constant attempt to be utterly truthful with oneself, a constant sedulousness to keep oneself fit and bright for God's service, and to increase one's knowledge and powers, and a hidden persistent watchfulness of one's baser motives, a watch against fear and indolence, against vanity, against greed and lust, against envy, malice, and uncharitableness. To have found God truly does in itself make God's service one's essential motive, but these evils lurk in the shadows, in the lassitudes and unwary moments. No one escapes them altogether, there is no need for tragic moods on account of imperfections. We can no more serve God without blunders and set-backs than we can win battles without losing men. But the less of such loss the better. The servant of God must keep his mind as wide and sound and his motives as clean as he can, just as an operating surgeon must keep his nerves and muscles as fit and his hands as clean as he can. Neither may righteously evade exercise and regular washing—of mind as of hands. An incessant watchfulness of one's self and one's thoughts and the soundness of one's thoughts; cleanliness, clearness, a wariness against indolence and prejudice, careful truth, habitual frankness, fitness and steadfast work; these are the daily fundamental duties that every one who truly comes to God will, as a matter of course, set before himself.

5. THE INCREASING KINGDOM

Now of the more intimate and personal life of the believer it will be more convenient to write a little later. Let us for the present pursue the idea of this world-kingdom of God, to whose establishment he calls us. This kingdom is to be a peaceful and co-ordinated activity of all mankind upon certain divine ends. These, we conceive, are first, the maintenance of the racial life; secondly, the exploration of the external being of nature as it is and as it has been, that is to say history and science; thirdly, that exploration of inherent human possibility which is art; fourthly, that clarification of thought and knowledge which is philosophy; and finally, the progressive enlargement and development of the racial life under these lights, so that God may work through a continually better body of humanity and through better and better equipped minds, that he and our race may increase for ever, working unendingly upon the development of the powers of life and the mastery of the blind forces of matter throughout the deeps of space. He sets out with us, we are persuaded, to conquer ourselves and our world and the stars. And beyond the stars our eyes can as yet see nothing, our imaginations reach and fail. Beyond the limits of our understanding is the veiled Being of Fate, whose face is hidden from us. . . .

It may be that minds will presently appear among us of such a quality that the face of that Unknown will not be altogether hidden. . . .

But the business of such ordinary lives as ours is the setting up of this earthly kingdom of God. That is the form into which our lives must fall and our consciences adapt themselves.

Belief in God as the Invisible King brings with it almost necessarily a conception of this coming kingdom of God on earth. Each believer as he grasps this natural and immediate consequence of the faith that has come into his life will form at the same time a Utopian conception of this world changed in the direction of God's purpose. The vision will follow the realisation of God's true nature and purpose as a necessary second step. And he will begin to develop the latent citizen of this world-state in himself. He will fall in with the idea of the world-wide sanities of this new order being drawn over the warring outlines of the present, and of men falling out of relationship with the old order and into relationship with the new. Many men and women are already working to-day at tasks that belong essentially to God's kingdom, tasks that would be of the same essential nature if the world were now a theocracy; for example, they are doing or sustaining scientific research or education or creative art; they are making roads to bring men together, they are doctors working for the world's health, they are building homes, they are constructing machinery to save and increase the powers of men. . . .

Such men and women need only to change their orientation as men will change about at a work-table when the light that was coming in a little while ago from the southern windows, begins presently to come in chiefly from the west, to become open and confessed servants of God. This work that they were doing for ambition, or the love of men or the love of knowledge or what seemed the inherent impulse to the work itself, or for money or honour or country or king, they will realise they are doing for God and by the power of God. Self-transformation into a citizen of God's kingdom and a new realisation of all earthly politics as no more than the struggle to define and achieve the kingdom of God in the earth, follow on, without any need for a fresh spiritual impulse, from the moment when God and the believer meet and clasp one another.

This transfiguration of the world into a theocracy may seem a merely fantastic idea to anyone who comes to it freshly without such general theological preparation as the preceding pages have made. But to anyone who has been at the pains to clear his mind even a little from the obsession of existing but transitory things, it ceases to be a mere suggestion and becomes more and more manifestly the real future of mankind. From the phase of "so things should be," the mind will pass very rapidly to the realisation that "so things will be." Towards this the directive wills among men have been drifting more and more steadily and perceptibly and with fewer eddyings and retardations, for many centuries. The purpose of mankind will not be always thus confused and fragmentary. This dissemination of will-power is a phase. The age of the warring tribes and kingdoms and empires that began a hundred centuries or so ago, draws to its close. The kingdom of God on earth is not a metaphor, not a mere spiritual state, not a dream, not an uncertain project; it is the thing before us, it is the close and inevitable destiny of mankind.

In a few score years the faith of the true God will be spreading about the world. The few halting confessions of God that one hears here and there to-day, like that little twittering of birds which comes before the dawn, will have swollen to a choral unanimity. In but a few centuries the whole world will be openly, confessedly, preparing for the kingdom. In but a few centuries God will have led us out of the dark forest of these present wars and confusions into the open brotherhood of his rule.

6. WHAT IS MY PLACE IN THE KINGDOM?

This conception of the general life of mankind as a transformation at thousands of points of the confused, egotistical, proprietary, partisan, nationalist, life-wasting chaos of human life to-day into the coherent development of the world kingdom of God, provides the form into which everyone who comes to the knowledge of God will naturally seek to fit his every thought and activity. The material greeds, the avarice, fear, rivalries, and ignoble ambitions of a disordered world will be challenged and examined under one general question: "What am I in the kingdom of God?"

It has already been suggested that there is a great and growing number of occupations that belong already to God's kingdom, research, teaching, creative art, creative administration, cultivation, construction, maintenance, and the honest satisfaction of honest practical human needs. For such people conversion to the intimacy of God means at most a change in the spirit of their work, a refreshed energy, a clearer understanding, a new zeal, a completer disregard of gains and praises and promotion. Pay, honours, and the like cease to be the inducement of effort. Service, and service alone, is the criterion that the quickened conscience will recognise.

Most of such people will find themselves in positions in which service is mingled with activities of a baser sort, in which service is a little warped and deflected by old traditions and usage, by mercenary and commercial considerations, by some inherent or special degradation of purpose. The spirit of God will not let the believer rest until his life is readjusted and as far as possible freed from the waste of these base diversions. For example a scientific investigator, lit and inspired by great inquiries, may be hampered by the conditions of his professorship or research fellowship, which exact an appearance of "practical" results. Or he may be obliged to lecture or conduct classes. He may be able to give but half his possible gift to the work of his real aptitude, and that at a sacrifice of money and reputation among short-sighted but influential contemporaries. Well, if he is by nature an investigator he will know that the research is what God needs of him. He cannot continue it at all if he leaves his position, and so he must needs waste something of his gift to save the rest. But should a poorer or a humbler post offer him better opportunity, there lies his work for God. There one has a very common and simple type of the problems that will arise in the lives of men when they are lit by sudden realisation of the immediacy of God.

Akin to that case is the perplexity of any successful physician between the increase of knowledge and the public welfare on the one hand, and the lucrative possibilities of his practice among wealthy people on the other. He belongs to a profession that is crippled by a mediaeval code, a profession which was blind to the common interest of the Public Health and regarded its members merely as skilled practitioners employed to "cure" individual ailments. Very slowly and tortuously do the methods of the profession adapt themselves to the modern conception of an army of devoted men working as a whole under God for the health of mankind as a whole, broadening out from the frowsy den of the "leech," with its crocodile and bottles and hieroglyphic prescriptions, to a skilled and illuminating co-operation with those who deal with the food and housing and economic life of the community.

And again quite parallel with these personal problems is the trouble of the artist between the market and vulgar fame on the one hand and his divine impulse on the other.

The presence of God will be a continual light and help in every decision that must be made by men and women in these more or less vitiated, but still fundamentally useful and righteous, positions.

The trouble becomes more marked and more difficult in the case of a man who is a manufacturer or a trader, the financier of business enterprise or the proprietor of great estates. The world is in need of manufactures and that goods should be distributed; land must be administered and new economic possibilities developed. The drift of things is in the direction of state ownership and control, but in a great number of cases the state is not ripe for such undertakings, it commands neither sufficient integrity nor sufficient ability, and the proprietor of factory, store, credit or land, must continue in possession, holding as a trustee for God and, so far as lies in his power, preparing for his supersession by some more public administration. Modern religion admits of no facile flights from responsibility. It permits no headlong resort to the wilderness and sterile virtue. It counts the recluse who fasts among scorpions in a cave as no better than a deserter in hiding. It unhesitatingly forbids any rich young man to sell all that he has and give to the poor. Himself and all that he has must be alike dedicated to God.

The plain duty that will be understood by the proprietor of land and of every sort of general need and service, so soon as he becomes aware of God, is so to administer his possessions as to achieve the maximum of possible efficiency, the most generous output, and the least private profit. He may set aside a salary for his maintenance; the rest he must deal with like a zealous public official. And if he perceives that the affair could be better administered by other hands than his own, then it is his business to get it into those hands with the smallest delay and the least profit to himself. . . .

The rights and wrongs of human equity are very different from right and wrong in the sight of God. In the sight of God no landlord has a RIGHT to his rent, no usurer has a RIGHT to his interest. A man is not justified in drawing the profits from an advantageous agreement nor free to spend the profits of a speculation as he will. God takes no heed of savings nor of abstinence. He recognises no right to the "rewards of abstinence," no right to any rewards. Those profits and comforts and consolations are the inducements that dangle before the eyes of the spiritually blind. Wealth is an embarrassment to the religious, for God calls them to account for it. The servant of God has no business with wealth or power except to use them immediately in the service of God. Finding these things in his hands he is bound to administer them in the service of God.

The tendency of modern religion goes far beyond the alleged communism of the early Christians, and far beyond the tithes of the scribes and Pharisees. God takes all. He takes you, blood and bones and house and acres, he takes skill and influence and expectations. For all the rest of your life you are nothing but God's agent. If you are not prepared for so complete a surrender, then you are infinitely remote from God. You must go your way. Here you are merely a curious interloper. Perhaps you have been desiring God as an experience, or coveting him as a possession. You have not begun to understand. This that we are discussing in this book is as yet nothing for you.

7. ADJUSTING LIFE

This picturing of a human world more to the mind of God than this present world and the discovery and realisation of one's own place and work in and for that kingdom of God, is the natural next phase in the development of the believer. He will set about revising and adjusting his scheme of life, his ways of living, his habits and his relationships in the light of his new convictions.

Most men and women who come to God will have already a certain righteousness in their lives; these things happen like a thunderclap only in strange exceptional cases, and the same movements of the mind that have brought them to God will already have brought their lives into a certain rightness of direction and conduct. Yet occasionally there will be someone to whom the self-examination that follows conversion will reveal an entirely wrong and evil way of living. It may be that the light has come to some rich idler doing nothing but follow a pleasurable routine. Or to someone following some highly profitable and amusing, but socially useless or socially mischievous occupation. One may be an advocate at the disposal of any man's purpose, or an actor or actress ready to fall in with any theatrical enterprise. Or a woman may find herself a prostitute or a pet wife, a mere kept instrument of indulgence. These are lives of prey, these are lives of futility; the light of God will not tolerate such lives. Here religion can bring nothing but a severance from the old way of life altogether, a break and a struggle towards use and service and dignity.

But even here it does not follow that because a life has been wrong the new life that begins must be far as the poles asunder from the old. Every sort of experience that has ever come to a human being is in the self that he brings to God, and there is no reason why a knowledge of evil ways should not determine the path of duty. No one can better devise protections against vices than those who have practised them; none know temptations better than those who have fallen. If a man has followed an evil trade, it becomes him to use his knowledge of the tricks of that trade to help end it. He knows the charities it may claim and the remedies it needs. . . .

A very interesting case to discuss in relation to this question of adjustment is that of the barrister. A practising barrister under contemporary conditions does indeed give most typically the opportunity for examining the relation of an ordinary self-respecting worldly life, to life under the dispensation of God discovered. A barrister is usually a man of some energy and ambition, his honour is moulded by the traditions of an ancient and antiquated profession, instinctively self-preserving and yet with a real desire for consistency and respect. As a profession it has been greedy and defensively conservative, but it has never been shameless nor has it ever broken faith with its own large and selfish, but quite definite, propositions. It has never for instance had the shamelessness of such a traditionless and undisciplined class as the early factory organisers. It has never had the dull incoherent wickedness of the sort of men who exploit drunkenness and the turf. It offends within limits. Barristers can be, and are, disbarred. But it is now a profession extraordinarily out of date; its code of honour derives from a time of cruder and lower conceptions of human relationship. It apprehends the State as a mere "ring" kept about private disputations; it has not begun to move towards the modern conception of the collective enterprise as the determining criterion of human conduct. It sees its business as a mere play upon the rules of a game between man and man, or between men and men. They haggle, they dispute, they inflict and suffer wrongs, they evade dues, and are liable or entitled to penalties and compensations. The primary business of the law is held to be decision in these wrangles, and as wrangling is subject to artistic elaboration, the business of the barrister is the business of a professional wrangler; he is a bravo in wig and gown who fights the duels of ordinary men because they are incapable, very largely on account of the complexities of legal procedure, of fighting for themselves. His business is never to explore any fundamental right in the matter. His business is to say all that can be said for his client, and to conceal or minimise whatever can be said against his client. The successful promoted advocate, who in Britain and the United States of America is the judge, and whose habits and interests all incline him to disregard the realities of the case in favour of the points in the forensic game, then adjudicates upon the contest. . . .

Now this condition of things is clearly incompatible with the modern conception of the world as becoming a divine kingdom. When the world is openly and confessedly the kingdom of God, the law court will exist only to adjust the differing views of men as to the manner of their service to God; the only right of action one man will have against another will be that he has been prevented or hampered or distressed by the other in serving God. The idea of the law court will have changed entirely from a place of dispute, exaction and vengeance, to a place of adjustment. The individual or some state organisation will plead ON BEHALF OF THE COMMON GOOD either against some state official or state regulation, or against the actions or inaction of another individual. This is the only sort of legal proceedings compatible with the broad beliefs of the new faith. . . . Every religion that becomes ascendant, in so far as it is not otherworldly, must necessarily set its stamp upon the methods and administration of the law. That this was not the case with Christianity is one of the many contributory aspects that lead one to the conviction that it was not Christianity that took possession of the Roman empire, but an imperial adventurer who took possession of an all too complaisant Christianity.

Reverting now from these generalisations to the problem of the religious from which they arose, it will have become evident that the essential work of anyone who is conversant with the existing practice and literature of the law and whose natural abilities are forensic, will lie in the direction of reconstructing the theory and practice of the law in harmony with modern conceptions, of making that theory and practice clear and plain to ordinary men, of reforming the abuses of the profession by working for the separation of bar and judiciary, for the amalgamation of the solicitors and the barristers, and the like needed reforms. These are matters that will probably only be properly set right by a quickening of conscience among lawyers themselves. Of no class of men is the help and service so necessary to the practical establishment of God's kingdom, as of men learned and experienced in the law. And there is no reason why for the present an advocate should not continue to plead in the courts, provided he does his utmost only to handle cases in which he believes he can serve the right. Few righteous cases are ill-served by a frank disposition on the part of lawyer and client to put everything before the court. Thereby of course there arises a difficult case of conscience. What if a lawyer, believing his client to be in the right, discovers him to be in the wrong? He cannot throw up the case unless he has been scandalously deceived, because so he would betray the confidence his client has put in him to "see him through." He has a right to "give himself away," but not to "give away" his client in this fashion. If he has a chance of a private consultation I think he ought to do his best to make his client admit the truth of the case and give in, but failing this he has no right to be virtuous on behalf of another. No man may play God to another; he may remonstrate, but that is the limit of his right. He must respect a confidence, even if it is purely implicit and involuntary. I admit that here the barrister is in a cleft stick, and that he must see the business through according to the confidence his client has put in him—and afterwards be as sorry as he may be if an injustice ensues. And also I would suggest a lawyer may with a fairly good conscience defend a guilty man as if he were innocent, to save him from unjustly heavy penalties. . . .

This comparatively full discussion of the barrister's problem has been embarked upon because it does bring in, in a very typical fashion, just those uncertainties and imperfections that abound in real life. Religious conviction gives us a general direction, but it stands aside from many of these entangled struggles in the jungle of conscience. Practice is often easier than a rule. In practice a lawyer will know far more accurately than a hypothetical case can indicate, how far he is bound to see his client through, and how far he may play the keeper of his client's conscience. And nearly every day there happens instances where the most subtle casuistry will fail and the finger of conscience point unhesitatingly. One may have worried long in the preparation and preliminaries of the issue, one may bring the case at last into the final court of conscience in an apparently hopeless tangle. Then suddenly comes decision.

The procedure of that silent, lit, and empty court in which a man states his case to God, is very simple and perfect. The excuses and the special pleading shrivel and vanish. In a little while the case lies bare and plain.

8. THE OATH OF ALLEGIANCE

The question of oaths of allegiance, acts of acquiescence in existing governments, and the like, is one that arises at once with the acceptance of God as the supreme and real King of the Earth. At the worst Caesar is a usurper, a satrap claiming to be sovereign; at the best he is provisional. Modern casuistry makes no great trouble for the believing public official. The chief business of any believer is to do the work for which he is best fitted, and since all state affairs are to become the affairs of God's kingdom it is of primary importance that they should come into the hands of God's servants. It is scarcely less necessary to a believing man with administrative gifts that he should be in the public administration, than that he should breathe and eat. And whatever oath or the like to usurper church or usurper king has been set up to bar access to service, is an oath imposed under duress. If it cannot be avoided it must be taken rather than that a man should become unserviceable. All such oaths are unfair and foolish things. They exclude no scoundrels; they are appeals to superstition. Whenever an opportunity occurs for the abolition of an oath, the servant of God will seize it, but where the oath is unavoidable he will take it.

The service of God is not to achieve a delicate consistency of statement; it is to do as much as one can of God's work.

9. THE PRIEST AND THE CREED

It may be doubted if this line of reasoning regarding the official and his oath can be extended to excuse the priest or pledged minister of religion who finds that faith in the true God has ousted his formal beliefs.

This has been a frequent and subtle moral problem in the intellectual life of the last hundred years. It has been increasingly difficult for any class of reading, talking, and discussing people such as are the bulk of the priesthoods of the Christian churches to escape hearing and reading the accumulated criticism of the Trinitarian theology and of the popularly accepted story of man's fall and salvation. Some have no doubt defeated this universal and insidious critical attack entirely, and honestly established themselves in a right-down acceptance of the articles and disciplines to which they have subscribed and of the creeds they profess and repeat. Some have recanted and abandoned their positions in the priesthood. But a great number have neither resisted the bacillus of criticism nor left the churches to which they are attached. They have adopted compromises, they have qualified their creeds with modifying footnotes of essential repudiation; they have decided that plain statements are metaphors and have undercut, transposed, and inverted the most vital points of the vulgarly accepted beliefs. One may find within the Anglican communion, Arians, Unitarians, Atheists, disbelievers in immortality, attenuators of miracles; there is scarcely a doubt or a cavil that has not found a lodgment within the ample charity of the English Establishment. I have been interested to hear one distinguished Canon deplore that "they" did not identify the Logos with the third instead of the second Person of the Trinity, and another distinguished Catholic apologist declare his indifference to the "historical Jesus." Within most of the Christian communions one may believe anything or nothing, provided only that one does not call too public an attention to one's eccentricity. The late Rev. Charles Voysey, for example, preached plainly in his church at Healaugh against the divinity of Christ, unhindered.

It was only when he published his sermons under the provocative title of "The Sling and the Stone," and caused an outcry beyond the limits of his congregation, that he was indicted and deprived.

Now the reasons why these men do not leave the ministry or priesthood in which they find themselves are often very plausible. It is probable that in very few cases is the retention of stipend or incumbency a conscious dishonesty. At the worst it is mitigated by thought for wife or child. It has only been during very exceptional phases of religious development and controversy that beliefs have been really sharp. A creed, like a coin, it may be argued, loses little in practical value because it is worn, or bears the image of a vanished king. The religious life is a reality that has clothed itself in many garments, and the concern of the priest or minister is with the religious life and not with the poor symbols that may indeed pretend to express, but do as a matter of fact no more than indicate, its direction. It is quite possible to maintain that the church and not the creed is the real and valuable instrument of religion, that the religious life is sustained not by its propositions but by its routines. Anyone who seeks the intimate discussion of spiritual things with professional divines, will find this is the substance of the case for the ecclesiastical sceptic. His church, he will admit, mumbles its statement of truth, but where else is truth? What better formulae are to be found for ineffable things? And meanwhile—he does good.

That may be a valid defence before a man finds God. But we who profess the worship and fellowship of the living God deny that religion is a matter of ineffable things. The way of God is plain and simple and easy to understand.

Therewith the whole position of the conforming sceptic is changed. If a professional religious has any justification at all for his professionalism it is surely that he proclaims the nearness and greatness of God. And these creeds and articles and orthodoxies are not proclamations but curtains, they are a darkening and confusion of what should be crystal clear. What compensatory good can a priest pretend to do when his primary business is the truth and his method a lie? The oaths and incidental conformities of men who wish to serve God in the state are on a different footing altogether from the falsehood and mischief of one who knows the true God and yet recites to a trustful congregation, foists upon a trustful congregation, a misleading and ill-phrased Levantine creed.

Such is the line of thought which will impose the renunciation of his temporalities and a complete cessation of services upon every ordained priest and minister as his first act of faith. Once that he has truly realised God, it becomes impossible for him ever to repeat his creed again. His course seems plain and clear. It becomes him to stand up before the flock he has led in error, and to proclaim the being and nature of the one true God. He must be explicit to the utmost of his powers. Then he may await his expulsion. It may be doubted whether it is sufficient for him to go away silently, making false excuses or none at all for his retreat. He has to atone for the implicit acquiescences of his conforming years.

10. THE UNIVERSALISM OF GOD

Are any sorts of people shut off as if by inherent necessity from God?

This is, so to speak, one of the standing questions of theology; it reappears with slight changes of form at every period of religious interest, it is for example the chief issue between the Arminian and the Calvinist. From its very opening proposition modern religion sweeps past and far ahead of the old Arminian teachings of Wesleyans and Methodists, in its insistence upon the entirely finite nature of God. Arminians seem merely to have insisted that God has conditioned himself, and by his own free act left men free to accept or reject salvation. To the realist type of mind—here as always I use "realist" in its proper sense as the opposite of nominalist—to the old-fashioned, over-exact and over-accentuating type of mind, such ways of thinking seem vague and unsatisfying. Just as it distresses the more downright kind of intelligence with a feeling of disloyalty to admit that God is not Almighty, so it troubles the same sort of intelligence to hear that there is no clear line to be drawn between the saved and the lost. Realists like an exclusive flavour in their faith. Moreover, it is a natural weakness of humanity to be forced into extreme positions by argument. It is probable, as I have already suggested, that the absolute attributes of God were forced upon Christianity under the stresses of propaganda, and it is probable that the theory of a super-human obstinancy beyond salvation arose out of the irritations natural to theological debate. It is but a step from the realisation that there are people absolutely unable or absolutely unwilling to see God as we see him, to the conviction that they are therefore shut off from God by an invincible soul blindness.

It is very easy to believe that other people are essentially damned.

Beyond the little world of our sympathies and comprehension

there are those who seem inaccessible to God by any means within our experience. They are people answering to the "hard-hearted," to the "stiff-necked generation" of the Hebrew prophets. They betray and even confess to standards that seem hopelessly base to us. They show themselves incapable of any disinterested enthusiasm for beauty or truth or goodness. They are altogether remote from intelligent sacrifice. To every test they betray vileness of texture; they are mean, cold, wicked. There are people who seem to cheat with a private self-approval, who are ever ready to do harsh and cruel things, whose use for social feeling is the malignant boycott, and for prosperity, monopolisation and humiliating display; who seize upon religion and turn it into persecution, and upon beauty to torment it on the altars of some joyless vice. We cannot do with such souls; we have no use for them, and it is very easy indeed to step from that persuasion to the belief that God has no use for them.

And besides these base people there are the stupid people and the people with minds so poor in texture that they cannot even grasp the few broad and simple ideas that seem necessary to the salvation we experience, who lapse helplessly into fetishistic and fearful conceptions of God, and are apparently quite incapable of distinguishing between what is practically and what is spiritually good.

It is an easy thing to conclude that the only way to God is our way to God, that he is the privilege of a finer and better sort to which we of course belong; that he is no more the God of the card-sharper or the pickpocket or the "smart" woman or the loan-monger or the village oaf than he is of the swine in the sty. But are we justified in thus limiting God to the measure of our moral and intellectual understandings? Because some people seem to me steadfastly and consistently base or hopelessly and incurably dull and confused, does it follow that there are not phases, albeit I have never chanced to see them, of exaltation in the one case and illumination in the other? And may I not be a little restricting my perception of Good? While I have been ready enough to pronounce this or that person as being, so far as I was concerned, thoroughly damnable or utterly dull, I find a curious reluctance to admit the general proposition which is necessary for these instances. It is possible that the difference between Arminian and Calvinist is a difference of essential intellectual temperament rather than of theoretical conviction. I am temperamentally Arminian as I am temperamentally Nominalist. I feel that it must be in the nature of God to attempt all souls. There must be accessibilities I can only suspect, and accessibilities of which I know nothing.

Yet here is a consideration pointing rather the other way. If you think, as you must think, that you yourself can be lost to God and damned, then I cannot see how you can avoid thinking that other people can be damned. But that is not to believe that there are people damned at the outset by their moral and intellectual insufficiency; that is not to make out that there is a class of essential and incurable spiritual defectives. The religious life preceded clear religious understanding and extends far beyond its range.

In my own case I perceive that in spite of the value I attach to true belief, the reality of religion is not an intellectual thing. The essential religious fact is in another than the mental sphere. I am passionately anxious to have the idea of God clear in my own mind, and to make my beliefs plain and clear to other people, and particularly to other people who may seem to be feeling with me; I do perceive that error is evil if only because a faith based on confused conceptions and partial understandings may suffer irreparable injury through the collapse of its substratum of ideas. I doubt if faith can be complete and enduring if it is not secured by the definite knowledge of the true God. Yet I have also to admit that I find the form of my own religious emotion paralleled by people with whom I have no intellectual sympathy and no agreement in phrase or formula at all.

There is for example this practical identity of religious feeling and this discrepancy of interpretation between such an inquirer as myself and a convert of the Salvation Army. Here, clothing itself in phrases and images of barbaric sacrifice, of slaughtered lambs and fountains of precious blood, a most repulsive and incomprehensible idiom to me, and expressing itself by shouts, clangour, trumpeting, gesticulations, and rhythmic pacings that stun and dismay my nerves, I find, the same object sought, release from self, and the same end, the end of identification with the immortal, successfully if perhaps rather insecurely achieved. I see God indubitably present in these excitements, and I see personalities I could easily have misjudged as too base or too dense for spiritual understandings, lit by the manifest reflection of divinity. One may be led into the absurdest underestimates of religious possibilities if one estimates people only coldly and in the light of everyday life. There is a sub-intellectual religious life which, very conceivably, when its utmost range can be examined, excludes nothing human from religious cooperation, which will use any words to its tune, which takes its phrasing ready-made from the world about it, as it takes the street for its temple, and yet which may be at its inner point in the directest contact with God. Religion may suffer from aphasia and still be religion; it may utter misleading or nonsensical words and yet intend and convey the truth. The methods of the Salvation Army are older than doctrinal Christianity, and may long survive it. Men and women may still chant of Beulah Land and cry out in the ecstasy of salvation; the tambourine, that modern revival of the thrilling Alexandrine sistrum, may still stir dull nerves to a first apprehension of powers and a call beyond the immediate material compulsion of life, when the creeds of Christianity are as dead as the lore of the Druids.

The emancipation of mankind from obsolete theories and formularies may be accompanied by great tides of moral and emotional release among types and strata that by the standards of a trained and explicit intellectual, may seem spiritually hopeless. It is not necessary to imagine the whole world critical and lucid in order to imagine the whole world unified in religious sentiment, comprehending the same phrases and coming together regardless of class and race and quality, in the worship and service of the true God. The coming kingship of God if it is to be more than hieratic tyranny must have this universality of appeal. As the head grows clear the body will turn in the right direction. To the mass of men modern religion says, "This is the God it has always been in your nature to apprehend."

11. GOD AND THE LOVE AND STATUS OF WOMEN

Now that we are discussing the general question of individual conduct, it will be convenient to take up again and restate in that relationship, propositions already made very plainly in the second and third chapters. Here there are several excellent reasons for a certain amount of deliberate repetition. . . .

All the mystical relations of chastity, virginity, and the like with religion, those questions of physical status that play so large a part in most contemporary religions, have disappeared from modern faith. Let us be as clear as possible upon this. God is concerned by the health and fitness and vigour of his servants; we owe him our best and utmost; but he has no special concern and no special preferences or commandments regarding sexual things.

Christ, it is manifest, was of the modern faith in these matters, he welcomed the Magdalen, neither would he condemn the woman taken in adultery. Manifestly corruption and disease were not to stand between him and those who sought God in him. But the Christianity of the creeds, in this as in so many respects, does not rise to the level of its founder, and it is as necessary to repeat to-day as though the name of Christ had not been ascendant for nineteen centuries, that sex is a secondary thing to religion, and sexual status of no account in the presence of God. It follows quite logically that God does not discriminate between man and woman in any essential things. We leave our individuality behind us when we come into the presence of God. Sex is not disavowed but forgotten. Just as one's last meal is forgotten—which also is a difference between the religious moment of modern faith and certain Christian sacraments. You are a believer and God is at hand to you; heed not your state; reach out to him and he is there. In the moment of religion you are human; it matters not what else you are, male or female, clean or unclean, Hebrew or Gentile, bond or free. It is AFTER the moment of religion that we become concerned about our state and the manner in which we use ourselves.

We have to follow our reason as our sole guide in our individual treatment of all such things as food and health and sex. God is the king of the whole world, he is the owner of our souls and bodies and all things. He is not particularly concerned about any aspect, because he is concerned about every aspect. We have to make the best use of ourselves for his kingdom; that is our rule of life. That rule means neither painful nor frantic abstinences nor any forced way of living. Purity, cleanliness, health, none of these things are for themselves, they are for use; none are magic, all are means. The sword must be sharp and clean. That does not mean that we are perpetually to sharpen and clean it—which would weaken and waste the blade. The sword must neither be drawn constantly nor always rusting in its sheath. Those who have had the wits and soul to come to God, will have the wits and soul to find out and know what is waste, what is vanity, what is the happiness that begets strength of body and spirit, what is error, where vice begins, and to avoid and repent and recoil from all those things that degrade. These are matters not of the rule of life but of the application of life. They must neither be neglected nor made disproportionally important.

To the believer, relationship with God is the supreme relationship. It is difficult to imagine how the association of lovers and friends can be very fine and close and good unless the two who love are each also linked to God, so that through their moods and fluctuations and the changes of years they can be held steadfast by his undying steadfastness. But it has been felt by many deep-feeling people that there is so much kindred between the love and trust of husband and wife and the feeling we have for God, that it is reasonable to consider the former also as a sacred thing. They do so value that close love of mated man and woman, they are so intent upon its permanence and completeness and to lift the dear relationship out of the ruck of casual and transitory things, that they want to bring it, as it were, into the very presence and assent of God. There are many who dream and desire that they are as deeply and completely mated as this, many more who would fain be so, and some who are. And from this comes the earnest desire to make marriage sacramental and the attempt to impose upon all the world the outward appearance, the restrictions, the pretence at least of such a sacramental union.

There may be such a quasi-sacramental union in many cases, but only after years can one be sure of it; it is not to be brought about by vows and promises but by an essential kindred and cleaving of body and spirit; and it concerns only the two who can dare to say they have it, and God. And the divine thing in marriage, the thing that is most like the love of God, is, even then, not the relationship of the man and woman as man and woman but the comradeship and trust and mutual help and pity that joins them. No doubt that from the mutual necessities of bodily love and the common adventure, the necessary honesties and helps of a joint life, there springs the stoutest, nearest, most enduring and best of human companionship; perhaps only upon that root can the best of mortal comradeship be got; but it does not follow that the mere ordinary coming together and pairing off of men and women is in itself divine or sacramental or anything of the sort. Being in love is a condition that may have its moments of sublime exaltation, but it is for the most part an experience far down the scale below divine experience; it is often love only in so far as it shares the name with better things; it is greed, it is admiration, it is desire, it is the itch for excitement, it is the instinct for competition, it is lust, it is curiosity, it is adventure, it is jealousy, it is hate. On a hundred scores 'lovers' meet and part. Thereby some few find true love and the spirit of God in themselves or others.

Lovers may love God in one another; I do not deny it. That is no reason why the imitation and outward form of this great happiness should be made an obligation upon all men and women who are attracted by one another, nor why it should be woven into the essentials of religion. For women much more than for men is this confusion dangerous, lest a personal love should shape and dominate their lives instead of God. "He for

God only; she for God in him," phrases the idea of Milton and of ancient Islam; it is the formula of sexual infatuation, a formula quite easily inverted, as the end of Goethe's Faust ("The woman soul leadeth us upward and on") may witness. The whole drift of modern religious feeling is against this exaggeration of sexual feeling, these moods of sexual slavishness, in spiritual things. Between the healthy love of ordinary mortal lovers in love and the love of God, there is an essential contrast and opposition in this, that preference, exclusiveness, and jealousy seem to be in the very nature of the former and are absolutely incompatible with the latter. The former is the intensest realisation of which our individualities are capable; the latter is the way of escape from the limitations of individuality. It may be true that a few men and more women do achieve the completest unselfishness and self-abandonment in earthly love. So the poets and romancers tell us. If so, it is that by an imaginative perversion they have given to some attractive person a worship that should be reserved for God and a devotion that is normally evoked only by little children in their mother's heart. It is not the way between most of the men and women one meets in this world.

But between God and the believer there is no other way, there is nothing else, but self-surrender and the ending of self.

CHAPTER THE SIXTH

MODERN IDEAS OF SIN AND DAMNATION

1. THE BIOLOGICAL EQUIVALENT OF SIN

If the reader who is unfamiliar with scientific things will obtain and read Metchnikoff's "Nature of Man," he will find there an interesting summary of the biological facts that bear upon and destroy the delusion that there is such a thing as individual perfection, that there is even ideal perfection for humanity. With an abundance of convincing instances Professor Metchnikoff demonstrates that life is a system of "disharmonies," capable of no perfect way, that there is no "perfect" dieting, no "perfect" sexual life, no "perfect" happiness, no "perfect" conduct. He releases one from the arbitrary but all too easy assumption that there is even an ideal "perfection" in organic life. He sweeps out of the mind with all the confidence and conviction of a physiological specialist, any idea that there is a perfect man or a conceivable perfect man. It is in the nature of every man to fall short at every point from perfection. From the biological point of view we are as individuals a series of involuntary "tries" on the part of an imperfect species towards an unknown end.

Our spiritual nature follows our bodily as a glove follows a hand. We are disharmonious beings and salvation no more makes an end to the defects of our souls than it makes an end to the decay of our teeth or to those vestigial structures of our body that endanger our physical welfare. Salvation leaves us still disharmonious, and adds not an inch to our spiritual and moral stature.

2. WHAT IS DAMNATION?

Let us now take up the question of what is Sin? and what we mean by the term "damnation," in the light of this view of human reality. Most of the great world religions are as clear as Professor Metchnikoff that life in the world is a tangle of disharmonies, and in most cases they supply a more or less myth-like explanation, they declare that evil is one side of the conflict between Ahriman and Ormazd, or that it is the punishment of an act of disobedience, of the fall of man and world alike from a state of harmony. Their case, like his, is that THIS world is damned.

We do not find the belief that superposed upon the miseries of this world there are the still bitterer miseries of punishments after death, so nearly universal. The endless punishments of hell appear to be an exploit of theory; they have a superadded appearance even in the Christian system; the same common tendency to superlatives and absolutes that makes men ashamed to admit that God is finite, makes them seek to enhance the merits of their Saviour by the device of everlasting fire. Conquest over the sorrow of life and the fear of death do not seem to them sufficient for Christ's glory.

Now the turning round of the modern mind from a conception of the universe as something derived deductively from the past to a conception of it as something gathering itself adventurously towards the future, involves a release from the supposed necessity to tell a story and explain why. Instead comes the inquiry, "To what end?" We can say without mental discomfort, these disharmonies are here, this damnation is here—inexplicably. We can, without any distressful inquiry into ultimate origins, bring our minds to the conception of a spontaneous and developing God arising out of those stresses in our hearts and in the universe, and arising to overcome them. Salvation for the individual is escape from the individual distress at disharmony and the individual defeat by death, into the Kingdom of God. And damnation can be nothing more and nothing less than the failure or inability or disinclination to make that escape.

Something of that idea of damnation as a lack of the will for salvation has crept at a number of points into contemporary religious thought. It was the fine fancy of Swedenborg that the damned go to their own hells of their own accord. It underlies a queer poem, "Simpson," by that interesting essayist upon modern Christianity, Mr. Clutton Brock, which I have recently read. Simpson dies and goes to hell—it is rather like the Cromwell Road—and approves of it very highly, and then and then only is he completely damned. Not to realise that one can be damned is certainly to be damned; such is Mr. Brock's idea. It is his definition of damnation. Satisfaction with existing things is damnation. It is surrender to limitation; it is acquiescence in "disharmony"; it is making peace with that enemy against whom God fights for ever.

(But whether there are indeed Simpsons who acquiesce always and for ever remains for me, as I have already confessed in the previous chapter, a quite open question. My Arminian temperament turns me from the Calvinistic conclusion of Mr. Brock's satire.)

3. SIN IS NOT DAMNATION

Now the question of sin will hardly concern those damned and lost by nature, if such there be. Sin is not the same thing as damnation, as we have just defined damnation. Damnation is a state, but sin is an incident. One is an essential and the other an incidental separation from God. It is possible to sin without being damned; and to be damned is to be in a state when sin scarcely matters, like ink upon a blackamoor. You cannot have questions of more or less among absolute things.

It is the amazing and distressful discovery of every believer so soon as the first exaltation of belief is past, that one does not remain always in touch with God. At first it seems incredible that one should ever have any motive again that is not also God's motive. Then one finds oneself caught unawares by a base impulse. We discover that discontinuousness of our apparently homogeneous selves, the unincorporated and warring elements that seemed at first altogether absent from the synthesis of conversion. We are tripped up by forgetfulness, by distraction, by old habits, by tricks of appearance. There come dull patches of existence; those mysterious obliterations of one's finer sense that are due at times to the little minor poisons one eats or drinks, to phases of fatigue, ill-health and bodily disorder, or one is betrayed by some unanticipated storm of emotion, brewed deep in the animal being and released by any trifling accident, such as personal jealousy or lust, or one is relaxed by contentment into vanity. All these rebel forces of our ill-coordinated selves, all these "disharmonies," of the inner being, snatch us away from our devotion to God's service, carry us off to follies, offences, unkindness, waste, and leave us compromised, involved, and regretful, perplexed by a hundred difficulties we have put in our own way back to God.

This is the personal problem of Sin. Here prayer avails; here God can help us. From God comes the strength to repent and make such reparation as we can, to begin the battle again further back and lower down. From God comes the power to anticipate the struggle with one's rebel self, and to resist and prevail over it.

4. THE SINS OF THE INSANE

An extreme case is very serviceable in such a discussion as this.

It happens that the author carries on a correspondence with several lunatics in asylums. There is a considerable freedom of notepaper in these institutions; the outgoing letters are no doubt censored or selected in some way, but a proportion at any rate are allowed to go out to their addresses. As a journalist who signs his articles and as the author of various books of fiction, as a frequent NAME, that is, to any one much forced back upon reading, the writer is particularly accessible to this type of correspondent. The letters come, some manifesting a hopeless disorder that permits of no reply, but some being the expression of minds overlaid not at all offensively by a web of fantasy, and some (and these are the more touching ones and the ones that most concern us now) as sanely conceived and expressed as any letters could be. They are written by people living lives very like the lives of us who are called "sane," except that they lift to a higher excitement and fall to a lower depression, and that these extremer phases of mania or melancholia slip the leash of mental consistency altogether and take abnormal forms. They tap deep founts of impulse, such as we of the safer ways of mediocrity do but glimpse under the influence of drugs, or in dreams and rare moments of controllable extravagance. Then the insane become "glorious," or they become murderous, or they become suicidal. All these letter-writers in confinement have convinced their fellow-creatures by some extravagance that they are a danger to themselves or others.

The letters that come from such types written during their sane intervals, are entirely sane. Some, who are probably unaware— I think they should know—of the offences or possibilities that justify their incarceration, write with a certain resentment at their position; others are entirely acquiescent, but one or two complain of the neglect of friends and relations. But all are as manifestly capable of religion and of the religious life as any other intelligent persons during the lucid interludes that make up nine-tenths perhaps of their lives. . . . Suppose now one of these cases, and suppose that the infirmity takes the form of some cruel, disgusting, or destructive disposition that may become at times overwhelming, and you have our universal trouble with sinful tendency, as it were magnified for examination. It is clear that the mania which defines his position must be the primary if not the cardinal business in the life of a lunatic, but his problem with that is different not in kind but merely in degree from the problem of lusts, vanities, and weaknesses in what we call normal lives. It is an unconquered tract, a great rebel province in his being, which refuses to serve God and tries to prevent him serving God, and succeeds at times in wresting his capital out of his control. But his relationship to that is the same relationship as ours to the backward and insubordinate parishes, criminal slums, and disorderly houses in our own private texture.

It is clear that the believer who is a lunatic is, as it were, only the better part of himself. He serves God with this unconquered disposition in him, like a man who, whatever else he is and does, is obliged to be the keeper of an untrustworthy and wicked animal. His beast gets loose. His only resort is to warn those about him when he feels that jangling or excitement of the nerves which precedes its escapes, to limit its range, to place weapons beyond its reach. And there are plenty of human beings very much in his case, whose beasts have never got loose or have got caught back before their essential insanity was apparent. And there are those uncertifiable lunatics we call men and women of "impulse" and "strong passions." If perhaps they have more self-control than the really mad, yet it happens oftener with them that the whole intelligent being falls under the dominion of evil. The passion scarcely less than the obsession may darken the whole moral sky. Repentance and atonement; nothing less will avail them after the storm has passed, and the sedulous preparation of defences and palliatives against the return of the storm.

This discussion of the lunatic's case gives us indeed, usefully coarse and large, the lines for the treatment of every human weakness by the servants of God. A "weakness," just like the lunatic's mania, becomes a particular charge under God, a special duty for the person it affects. He has to minimise it, to isolate it, to keep it out of mischief. If he can he must adopt preventive measures. . . .

These passions and weaknesses that get control of us hamper our usefulness to God, they are an incessant anxiety and distress to us, they wound our self-respect and make us incomprehensible to many who would trust us, they discredit the faith we profess. If they break through and break through again it is natural and proper that men and women should cease to believe in our faith, cease to work with us or to meet us frankly. . . . Our sins do everything evil to us and through us except separate us from God.

Yet let there be no mistake about one thing. Here prayer is a power. Here God can indeed work miracles. A man with the light of God in his heart can defeat vicious habits, rise again combative and undaunted after a hundred falls, escape from the grip of lusts and revenges, make head against despair, thrust back the very onset of madness. He is still the same man he was before he came to God, still with his libidinous, vindictive, boastful, or indolent vein; but now his will to prevail over those qualities can refer to an exterior standard and an external interest, he can draw upon a strength, almost boundless, beyond his own.

5. BELIEVE, AND YOU ARE SAVED

But be a sin great or small, it cannot damn a man once he has found God. You may kill and hang for it, you may rob or rape; the moment you truly repent and set yourself to such atonement and reparation as is possible there remains no barrier between you and God. Directly you cease to hide or deny or escape, and turn manfully towards the consequences and the setting of things right, you take hold again of the hand of God. Though you sin seventy times seven times, God will still forgive the poor rest of you. Nothing but utter blindness of the spirit can shut a man off from God.

There is nothing one can suffer, no situation so unfortunate, that it can shut off one who has the thought of God, from God. If you but lift up your head for a moment out of a stormy chaos of madness and cry to him, God is there, God will not fail you. A convicted criminal, frankly penitent, and neither obdurate nor abject, whatever the evil of his yesterdays, may still die well and bravely on the gallows to the glory of God. He may step straight from that death into the immortal being of God.

This persuasion is the very essence of the religion of the true God. There is no sin, no state that, being regretted and repented of, can stand between God and man.

CHAPTER THE SEVENTH

THE IDEA OF A CHURCH

1. THE WORLD DAWN

As yet those who may be counted as belonging definitely to the new religion are few and scattered and unconfessed, their realisations are still uncertain and incomplete. But that is no augury for the continuance of this state of affairs even for the next few decades. There are many signs that the revival is coming very swiftly, it may be coming as swiftly as the morning comes after a tropical night. It may seem at present as though nothing very much were happening, except for the fact that the old familiar constellations of theology have become a little pallid and lost something of their multitude of points. But nothing fades of itself. The deep stillness of the late night is broken by a stirring, and the morning star of creedless faith, the last and brightest of the stars, the star that owes its light to the coming sun is in the sky.

There is a stirring and a movement. There is a stir, like the stir before a breeze. Men are beginning to speak of religion without the bluster of the Christian formulae; they have begun to speak of God without any reference to Omnipresence, Omniscience, Omnipotence. The Deists and Theists of an older generation, be it noted, never did that. Their "Supreme Being" repudiated nothing. He was merely the whittled stump of the Trinity. It is in the last few decades that the western mind has slipped loose from this absolutist conception of God that has dominated the intelligence of Christendom at least, for many centuries. Almost unconsciously the new thought is taking a course that will lead it far away from the moorings of Omnipotence. It is like a ship that has slipped its anchors and drifts, still sleeping, under the pale and vanishing stars, out to the open sea. . . .

2. CONVERGENT RELIGIOUS MOVEMENTS

In quite a little while the whole world may be alive with this renascent faith.

For emancipation from the Trinitarian formularies and from a belief in an infinite God means not merely a great revivification of minds trained under the decadence of orthodox Christianity, minds which have hitherto been hopelessly embarrassed by the choice between pseudo-Christian religion or denial, but also it opens the way towards the completest understanding and sympathy and participation with the kindred movements for release and for an intensification of the religious life, that are going on outside the sphere of the Christian tradition and influence altogether. Allusion has already been made to the sympathetic devotional poetry of Rabindranath Tagore; he stands for a movement in Brahminism parallel with and assimilable to the worship of the true God of mankind.

It is too often supposed that the religious tendency of the East is entirely towards other-worldness, to a treatment of this life as an evil entanglement and of death as a release and a blessing. It is too easily assumed that Eastern teaching is wholly concerned with renunciation, not merely of self but of being, with the escape from all effort of any sort into an exalted vacuity. This is indeed neither the spirit of China nor of Islam nor of the every-day life of any people in the world. It is not the spirit of the Sikh nor of these newer developments of Hindu thought. It has never been the spirit of Japan. To-day less than ever does Asia seem disposed to give up life and the effort of life. Just as readily as Europeans, do the Asiatics reach out their arms to that fuller life we can live, that greater intensity of existence, to which we can attain by escaping from ourselves. All mankind is seeking God. There is not a nation nor a city in the globe where men are not being urged at this moment by the spirit of God in them towards the discovery of God. This is not an age of despair but an age of hope in Asia as in all the world besides.

Islam is undergoing a process of revision closely parallel to that which ransacks Christianity. Tradition and mediaeval doctrines are being thrust aside in a similar way. There is much probing into the spirit and intention of the Founder. The time is almost ripe for a heart-searching Dialogue of the Dead, "How we settled our religions for ever and ever," between, let us say, Eusebius of Caesarea and one of Nizam-al-Mulk's tame theologians. They would be drawn together by the same tribulations; they would be in the closest sympathy against the temerity of the moderns; they would have a common courtliness. The Quran is but little read by Europeans; it is ignorantly supposed to contain many things that it does not contain; there is much confusion in people's minds between its text and the ancient Semitic traditions and usages retained by its followers; in places it may seem formless and barbaric; but what it has chiefly to tell of is the leadership of one individualised militant God who claims the rule of the whole world, who favours neither rank nor race, who would lead men to righteousness. It is much more free from sacramentalism, from vestiges of the ancient blood sacrifice, and its associated sacerdotalism, than Christianity. The religion that will presently sway mankind can be reached more easily from that starting-point than from the confused mysteries of Trinitarian theology. Islam was never saddled with a creed. With the very name "Islam" (submission to God) there is no quarrel for those who hold the new faith. . . .

All the world over there is this stirring in the dry bones of the old beliefs. There is scarcely a religion that has not its Bahaism, its Modernists, its Brahmo Somaj, its "religion without theology," its attempts to escape from old forms and hampering associations to that living and world-wide spiritual reality upon which the human mind almost instinctively insists. . . .

It is the same God we all seek; he becomes more and more plainly the same God.

So that all this religious stir, which seems so multifold and incidental and disconnected and confused and entirely ineffective to-day, may be and most probably will be, in quite a few years a great flood of religious unanimity pouring over and changing all human affairs, sweeping away the old priesthoods and tabernacles and symbols and shrines, the last crumb of the Orphic victim and the last rag of the Serapeum, and turning all men about into one direction, as the ships and houseboats swing round together in some great river with the uprush of the tide. . . .

3. CAN THERE BE A TRUE CHURCH?

Among those who are beginning to realise the differences and identities of the revived religion that has returned to them, certain questions of organisation and assembly are being discussed. Every new religious development is haunted by the precedents of the religion it replaces, and it was only to be expected that among those who have recovered their faith there should be a search for apostles and disciples, an attempt to determine sources and to form original congregations, especially among people with European traditions.

These dispositions mark a relapse from understanding. They are imitative. This time there has been no revelation here or there; there is no claim to a revelation but simply that God has become visible. Men have thought and sought until insensibly the fog of obsolete theology has cleared away. There seems no need therefore for special teachers or a special propaganda, or any ritual or observances that will seem to insist upon differences. The Christian precedent of a church is particularly misleading. The church with its sacraments and its sacerdotalism is the disease of Christianity. Save for a few doubtful interpolations there is no evidence that Christ tolerated either blood sacrifices or the mysteries of priesthood. All these antique grossnesses were superadded after his martyrdom. He preached not a cult but a gospel; he sent out not medicine men but apostles.

No doubt all who believe owe an apostolic service to God. They become naturally apostolic. As men perceive and realise God, each will be disposed in his own fashion to call his neighbour's attention to what he sees. The necessary elements of religion could be written on a post card; this book, small as it is, bulks large not by what it tells positively but because it deals with misconceptions. We may (little doubt have I that we do) need special propagandas and organisations to discuss errors and keep back the jungle of false ideas, to maintain free speech and restrain the enterprise of the persecutor, but we do not want a church to keep our faith for us. We want our faith spread, but for that there is no need for orthodoxies and controlling organisations of statement. It is for each man to follow his own impulse, and to speak to his like in his own fashion.

Whatever religious congregations men may form henceforth in the name of the true God must be for their own sakes and not to take charge of religion.

The history of Christianity, with its encrustation and suffocation in dogmas and usages, its dire persecutions of the faithful by the unfaithful, its desiccation and its unlovely decay, its invasion by robes and rites and all the tricks and vices of the Pharisees whom Christ detested and denounced, is full of warning against the dangers of a church. Organisation is an excellent thing for the material needs of men, for the draining of towns, the marshalling of traffic, the collecting of eggs, and the carrying of letters, the distribution of bread, the notification of measles, for hygiene and economics and suchlike affairs. The better we organise such things, the freer and better equipped we leave men's minds for nobler purposes, for those adventures and experiments towards God's purpose which are the reality of life. But all organisations must be watched, for whatever is organised can be "captured" and misused. Repentance, moreover, is the beginning and essential of the religious life, and organisations (acting through their secretaries and officials) never repent. God deals only with the individual for the individual's surrender. He takes no cognisance of committees.

Those who are most alive to the realities of living religion are most mistrustful of this congregating tendency. To gather together is to purchase a benefit at the price of a greater loss, to strengthen one's sense of brotherhood by excluding the majority of mankind. Before you know where you are you will have exchanged the spirit of God for ESPRIT DE CORPS. You will have reinvented the SYMBOL; you will have begun to keep anniversaries and establish sacramental ceremonies. The disposition to form cliques and exclude and conspire against unlike people is all too strong in humanity, to permit of its formal encouragement. Even such organisation as is implied by a creed is to be avoided, for all living faith coagulates as you phrase it. In this book I have not given so much as a definite name to the faith of the true God. Organisation for worship and collective exaltation also, it may be urged, is of little manifest good. You cannot appoint beforehand a time and place for God to irradiate your soul.

All these are very valid objections to the church-forming disposition.

4. ORGANISATIONS UNDER GOD

Yet still this leaves many dissatisfied. They want to shout out about God. They want to share this great thing with all mankind.

Why should they not shout and share?

Let them express all that they desire to express in their own fashion by themselves or grouped with their friends as they will. Let them shout chorally if they are so disposed. Let them work in a gang if so they can work the better. But let them guard themselves against the idea that they can have God particularly or exclusively with them in any such undertaking. Or that so they can express God rather than themselves.

That I think states the attitude of the modern spirit towards the idea of a church. Mankind passes for ever out of the idolatry of altars, away from the obscene rites of circumcision and symbolical cannibalism, beyond the sway of the ceremonial priest. But if the modern spirit holds that religion cannot be organised or any intermediary thrust between God and man, that does not preclude infinite possibilities of organisation and collective action UNDER God and within the compass of religion. There is no reason why religious men should not band themselves the better to attain specific ends. To borrow a term from British politics, there is no objection to AD HOC organisations. The objection lies not against subsidiary organisations for service but against organisations that may claim to be comprehensive.

For example there is no reason why one should not—and in many cases there are good reasons why one should—organise or join associations for the criticism of religious ideas, an employment that may pass very readily into propaganda.

Many people feel the need of prayer to resist the evil in

themselves and to keep them in mind of divine emotion. And many want not merely prayer but formal prayer and the support of others, praying in unison. The writer does not understand this desire or need for collective prayer very well, but there are people who appear to do so and there is no reason why they should not assemble for that purpose. And there is no doubt that divine poetry, divine maxims, religious thought finely expressed, may be heard, rehearsed, collected, published, and distributed by associations. The desire for expression implies a sort of assembly, a hearer at least as well as a speaker. And expression has many forms. People with a strong artistic impulse will necessarily want to express themselves by art when religion touches them, and many arts, architecture and the drama for example, are collective undertakings. I do not see why there should not be, under God, associations for building cathedrals and suchlike great still places urgent with beauty, into which men and women may go to rest from the clamour of the day's confusions; I do not see why men should not make great shrines and pictures expressing their sense of divine things, and why they should not combine in such enterprises rather than work to fill heterogeneous and chaotic art galleries. A wave of religious revival and religious clarification, such as I foresee, will most certainly bring with it a great revival of art, religious art, music, songs, and writings of all sorts, drama, the making of shrines, praying places, temples and retreats, the creation of pictures and sculptures. It is not necessary to have priestcraft and an organised church for such ends. Such enrichments of feeling and thought are part of the service of God.

And again, under God, there may be associations and fraternities for research in pure science; associations for the teaching and simplification of languages; associations for promoting and watching education; associations for the discussion of political problems and the determination of right policies. In all these ways men may multiply their use by union. Only when associations seek to control things of belief, to dictate formulae, restrict religious activities or the freedom of religious thought and teaching, when they tend to subdivide those who believe and to set up jealousies or exclusions, do they become antagonistic to the spirit of modern religion.

5. THE STATE IS GOD'S INSTRUMENT

Because religion cannot be organised, because God is everywhere and immediately accessible to every human being, it does not follow that religion cannot organise every other human affair. It is indeed essential to the idea that God is the Invisible King of this round world and all mankind, that we should see in every government, great and small, from the council of the world-state that is presently coming, down to the village assembly, the instrument of God's practical control. Religion which is free, speaking freely through whom it will, subject to a perpetual unlimited criticism, will be the life and driving power of the whole organised world. So that if you prefer not to say that there will be no church, if you choose rather to declare that the world-state is God's church, you may have it so if you will. Provided that you leave conscience and speech and writing and teaching about divine things absolutely free, and that you try to set no nets about God.

The world is God's and he takes it. But he himself remains freedom, and we find our freedom in him.

THE ENVOY

So I end this compact statement of the renascent religion which I believe to be crystallising out of the intellectual, social, and spiritual confusions of this time. It is an account rendered. It is a statement and record; not a theory. There is nothing in all this that has been invented or constructed by the writer; I have been but scribe to the spirit of my generation; I have at most assembled and put together things and thoughts that I have come upon, have transferred the statements of "science" into religious terminology, rejected obsolescent definitions, and re-coordinated propositions that had drifted into opposition. Thus, I see, ideas are developing, and thus have I written them down. It is a secondary matter that I am convinced that this trend of intelligent opinion is a discovery of truth. The reader is told of my own belief merely to avoid an affectation of impartiality and aloofness.

The theogony here set forth is ancient; one can trace it appearing and disappearing and recurring in the mutilated records of many different schools of speculation; the conception of God as finite is one that has been discussed very illuminatingly in recent years in the work of one I am happy to write of as my friend and master, that very great American, the late William James. It was an idea that became increasingly important to him towards the end of his life. And it is the most releasing idea in the system.

Only in the most general terms can I trace the other origins of these present views. I do not think modern religion owes much to what is called Deism or Theism. The rather abstract and futile Deism of the eighteenth century, of "votre Etre supreme" who bored the friends of Robespierre, was a sterile thing, it has little relation to these modern developments, it conceived of God as an infinite Being of no particular character whereas God is a finite being of a very especial character. On the other hand men and women who have set themselves, with unavoidable theological preconceptions, it is true, to speculate upon the actual teachings and quality of Christ, have produced interpretations that have interwoven insensibly with thoughts more apparently new. There is a curious modernity about very many of Christ's recorded sayings. Revived religion has also, no doubt, been the receiver of many religious bankruptcies, of Positivism for example, which failed through its bleak abstraction and an unspiritual texture. Religion, thus restated, must, I think, presently incorporate great sections of thought that are still attached to formal Christianity. The time is at hand when many of the organised Christian churches will be forced to define their positions, either in terms that will identify them with this renascence, or that will lead to the release of their more liberal adherents. Its probable obligations to Eastern thought are less readily estimated by a European writer.

Modern religion has no revelation and no founder; it is the privilege and possession of no coterie of disciples or exponents; it is appearing simultaneously round and about the world exactly as a crystallising substance appears here and there in a super-saturated solution. It is a process of truth, guided by the divinity in men. It needs no other guidance, and no protection. It needs nothing but freedom, free speech, and honest statement. Out of the most mixed and impure solutions a growing crystal is infallibly able to select its substance. The diamond arises bright, definite, and pure out of a dark matrix of structureless confusion.

This metaphor of crystallisation is perhaps the best symbol of the advent and growth of the new understanding. It has no church, no authorities, no teachers, no orthodoxy. It does not even thrust and struggle among the other things; simply it grows clear. There will be no putting an end to it. It arrives inevitably, and it will continue to separate itself out from confusing ideas. It becomes, as it were the Koh-i-noor; it is a Mountain of Light, growing and increasing. It is an all-pervading lucidity, a brightness and clearness. It has no head to smite, no body you can destroy; it overleaps all barriers; it breaks out in despite of every enclosure. It will compel all things to orient themselves to it.

It comes as the dawn comes, through whatever clouds and mists may be here or whatever smoke and curtains may be there. It comes as the day comes to the ships that put to sea.

It is the Kingdom of God at hand.

ABOUT THE AUTHOR

H.G. Wells (September 21, 1866 – August 13, 1946), born Herbert George Wells, was an English writer best known for such science fiction novels as The Time Machine, The War of the Worlds, The Invisible Man, and The Island of Doctor Moreau. He was a prolific writer of both fiction and non-fiction, and produced works in many different genres, including contemporary novels, history, and social commentary. He was also an outspoken socialist. His later works become increasingly political and didactic, and only his early science fiction novels are widely read today. Wells, along with Hugo Gernsback and Jules Verne, is sometimes referred to as "The Father of Science Fiction".

Herbert George Wells, the fifth and last child of Joseph Wells (a former domestic gardener and at the time shopkeeper and cricketer) and his wife Sarah Neal (a former domestic servant), was born at Atlas House, 47 High Street, Bromley, Kent. The family was of the impoverished lower-middle-class.

A defining incident of young Wells's life is said to be an accident he had in 1874, when he was seven years old, which left him bedridden with a broken leg. To pass the time he started reading, and soon became devoted to the other worlds and lives to which books gave him access; they also stimulated his desire to write.

Choose from Thousands of 1stWorldLibrary Classics By

A. M. Barnard
Ada Leverson
Adolphus William Ward
Aesop
Agatha Christie
Alexander Aaronsohn
Alexander Kielland
Alexandre Dumas
Alfred Gatty
Alfred Ollivant
Alice Duer Miller
Alice Turner Curtis
Alice Dunbar
Allen Chapman
Alleyne Ireland
Ambrose Bierce
Amelia E. Barr
Amory H. Bradford
Andrew Lang
Andrew McFarland Davis
Andy Adams
Angela Brazil
Anna Alice Chapin
Anna Sewell
Annie Besant
Annie Hamilton Donnell
Annie Payson Call
Annie Roe Carr
Annonaymous
Anton Chekhov
Archibald Lee Fletcher
Arnold Bennett
Arthur C. Benson
Arthur Conan Doyle
Arthur M. Winfield
Arthur Ransome
Arthur Schnitzler
Arthur Train
Atticus
B.H. Baden-Powell
B. M. Bower
B. C. Chatterjee
Baroness Emmuska Orczy
Baroness Orczy
Basil King
Bayard Taylor
Ben Macomber
Bertha Muzzy Bower
Bjornstjerne Bjornson

Booth Tarkington
Boyd Cable
Bram Stoker
C. Collodi
C. E. Orr
C. M. Ingleby
Carolyn Wells
Catherine Parr Traill
Charles A. Eastman
Charles Amory Beach
Charles Dickens
Charles Dudley Warner
Charles Farrar Browne
Charles Ives
Charles Kingsley
Charles Klein
Charles Hanson Towne
Charles Lathrop Pack
Charles Romyn Dake
Charles Whibley
Charles Willing Beale
Charlotte M. Braeme
Charlotte M. Yonge
Charlotte Perkins Stetson
Clair W. Hayes
Clarence Day Jr.
Clarence E. Mulford
Clemence Housman
Confucius
Coningsby Dawson
Cornelis DeWitt Wilcox
Cyril Burleigh
D. H. Lawrence
Daniel Defoe
David Garnett
Dinah Craik
Don Carlos Janes
Donald Keyhoe
Dorothy Kilner
Dougan Clark
Douglas Fairbanks
E. Nesbit
E. P. Roe
E. Phillips Oppenheim
E. S. Brooks
Earl Barnes
Edgar Rice Burroughs
Edith Van Dyne
Edith Wharton

Edward Everett Hale
Edward J. O'Biren
Edward S. Ellis
Edwin L. Arnold
Eleanor Atkins
Eleanor Hallowell Abbott
Eliot Gregory
Elizabeth Gaskell
Elizabeth McCracken
Elizabeth Von Arnim
Ellem Key
Emerson Hough
Emilie F. Carlen
Emily Bronte
Emily Dickinson
Enid Bagnold
Enilor Macartney Lane
Erasmus W. Jones
Ernie Howard Pie
Ethel May Dell
Ethel Turner
Ethel Watts Mumford
Eugene Sue
Eugenie Foa
Eugene Wood
Eustace Hale Ball
Evelyn Everett-green
Everard Cotes
F. H. Cheley
F. J. Cross
F. Marion Crawford
Fannie E. Newberry
Federick Austin Ogg
Ferdinand Ossendowski
Fergus Hume
Florence A. Kilpatrick
Fremont B. Deering
Francis Bacon
Francis Darwin
Frances Hodgson Burnett
Frances Parkinson Keyes
Frank Gee Patchin
Frank Harris
Frank Jewett Mather
Frank L. Packard
Frank V. Webster
Frederic Stewart Isham
Frederick Trevor Hill
Frederick Winslow Taylor

Friedrich Kerst	Hayden Carruth	James Branch Cabell
Friedrich Nietzsche	Helent Hunt Jackson	James DeMille
Fyodor Dostoyevsky	Helen Nicolay	James Joyce
G.A. Henty	Hendrik Conscience	James Lane Allen
G.K. Chesterton	Hendy David Thoreau	James Lane Allen
Gabrielle E. Jackson	Henri Barbusse	James Oliver Curwood
Garrett P. Serviss	Henrik Ibsen	James Oppenheim
Gaston Leroux	Henry Adams	James Otis
George A. Warren	Henry Ford	James R. Driscoll
George Ade	Henry Frost	Jane Abbott
Geroge Bernard Shaw	Henry James	Jane Austen
George Cary Eggleston	Henry Jones Ford	Jane L. Stewart
George Durston	Henry Seton Merriman	Janet Aldridge
George Ebers	Henry W Longfellow	Jens Peter Jacobsen
George Eliot	Herbert A. Giles	Jerome K. Jerome
George Gissing	Herbert Carter	Jessie Graham Flower
George MacDonald	Herbert N. Casson	John Buchan
George Meredith	Herman Hesse	John Burroughs
George Orwell	Hildegard G. Frey	John Cournos
George Sylvester Viereck	Homer	John F. Kennedy
George Tucker	Honore De Balzac	John Gay
George W. Cable	Horace B. Day	John Glasworthy
George Wharton James	Horace Walpole	John Habberton
Gertrude Atherton	Horatio Alger Jr.	John Joy Bell
Gordon Casserly	Howard Pyle	John Kendrick Bangs
Grace E. King	Howard R. Garis	John Milton
Grace Gallatin	Hugh Lofting	John Philip Sousa
Grace Greenwood	Hugh Walpole	John Taintor Foote
Grant Allen	Humphry Ward	Jonas Lauritz Idemil Lie
Guillermo A. Sherwell	Ian Maclaren	Jonathan Swift
Gulielma Zollinger	Inez Haynes Gillmore	Joseph A. Altsheler
Gustav Flaubert	Irving Bacheller	Joseph Carey
H. A. Cody	Isabel Cecilia Williams	Joseph Conrad
H. B. Irving	Isabel Hornibrook	Joseph E. Badger Jr
H.C. Bailey	Israel Abrahams	Joseph Hergesheimer
H. G. Wells	Ivan Turgenev	Joseph Jacobs
H. H. Munro	J.G.Austin	Jules Vernes
H. Irving Hancock	J. Henri Fabre	Julian Hawthrone
H. R. Naylor	J. M. Barrie	Julie A Lippmann
H. Rider Haggard	J. M. Walsh	Justin Huntly McCarthy
H. W. C. Davis	J. Macdonald Oxley	Kakuzo Okakura
Haldeman Julius	J. R. Miller	Karle Wilson Baker
Hall Caine	J. S. Fletcher	Kate Chopin
Hamilton Wright Mabie	J. S. Knowles	Kenneth Grahame
Hans Christian Andersen	J. Storer Clouston	Kenneth McGaffey
Harold Avery	J. W. Duffield	Kate Langley Bosher
Harold McGrath	Jack London	Kate Langley Bosher
Harriet Beecher Stowe	Jacob Abbott	Katherine Cecil Thurston
Harry Castlemon	James Allen	Katherine Stokes
Harry Coghill	James Andrews	L. A. Abbot
Harry Houidini	James Baldwin	L. T. Meade

L. Frank Baum	Owen Johnson	Stephen Crane
Latta Griswold	P.G. Wodehouse	Stewart Edward White
Laura Dent Crane	Paul and Mabel Thorne	Stijn Streuvels
Laura Lee Hope	Paul G. Tomlinson	Swami Abhedananda
Laurence Housman	Paul Severing	Swami Parmananda
Lawrence Beasley	Percy Brebner	T. S. Ackland
Leo Tolstoy	Percy Keese Fitzhugh	T. S. Arthur
Leonid Andreyev	Peter B. Kyne	The Princess Der Ling
Lewis Carroll	Plato	Thomas A. Janvier
Lewis Sperry Chafer	Quincy Allen	Thomas A Kempis
Lilian Bell	R. Derby Holmes	Thomas Anderton
Lloyd Osbourne	R. L. Stevenson	Thomas Bailey Aldrich
Louis Hughes	R. S. Ball	Thomas Bulfinch
Louis Joseph Vance	Rabindranath Tagore	Thomas De Quincey
Louis Tracy	Rahul Alvares	Thomas Dixon
Louisa May Alcott	Ralph Bonehill	Thomas H. Huxley
Lucy Fitch Perkins	Ralph Henry Barbour	Thomas Hardy
Lucy Maud Montgomery	Ralph Victor	Thomas More
Luther Benson	Ralph Waldo Emmerson	Thornton W. Burgess
Lydia Miller Middleton	Rene Descartes	U. S. Grant
Lyndon Orr	Ray Cummings	Upton Sinclair
M. Corvus	Rex Beach	Valentine Williams
M. H. Adams	Rex E. Beach	Various Authors
Margaret E. Sangster	Richard Harding Davis	Vaughan Kester
Margret Howth	Richard Jefferies	Victor Appleton
Margaret Vandercook	Richard Le Gallienne	Victor G. Durham
Margaret W. Hungerford	Robert Barr	Victoria Cross
Margret Penrose	Robert Frost	Virginia Woolf
Maria Edgeworth	Robert Gordon Anderson	Wadsworth Camp
Maria Thompson Daviess	Robert L. Drake	Walter Camp
Mariano Azuela	Robert Lansing	Walter Scott
Marion Polk Angellotti	Robert Lynd	Washington Irving
Mark Overton	Robert Michael Ballantyne	Wilbur Lawton
Mark Twain	Robert W. Chambers	Wilkie Collins
Mary Austin	Rosa Nouchette Carey	Willa Cather
Mary Catherine Crowley	Rudyard Kipling	Willard F. Baker
Mary Cole	Saint Augustine	William Dean Howells
Mary Hastings Bradley	Samuel B. Allison	William le Queux
Mary Roberts Rinehart	Samuel Hopkins Adams	W. Makepeace Thackeray
Mary Rowlandson	Sarah Bernhardt	William W. Walter
M. Wollstonecraft Shelley	Sarah C. Hallowell	William Shakespeare
Maud Lindsay	Selma Lagerlof	Winston Churchill
Max Beerbohm	Sherwood Anderson	Yei Theodora Ozaki
Myra Kelly	Sigmund Freud	Yogi Ramacharaka
Nathaniel Hawthrone	Standish O'Grady	Young E. Allison
Nicolo Machiavelli	Stanley Weyman	Zane Grey
O. F. Walton	Stella Benson	
Oscar Wilde	Stella M. Francis	

www.ingramcontent.com/pod-product-compliance
Lightning Source LLC
Chambersburg PA
CBHW020005050426
42450CB00005B/319